THE TRAVELLER'S POCKET COMPANION

by Georgina Newbery
and Rhiannon Guy

PAVILION

A Think Book for Pavilion Books

This edition published by Pavilion Books in 2007
First published in the United Kingdom in 2004 by Robson Books
10 Southcombe Street, London W14 0RA

Imprints of Anova Books Company Ltd

Text and design © Think Publishing 2004
The moral rights of the authors have been asserted

Edited by Georgina Newbery and Rhiannon Guy
The Companion team: Vicky Bamforth, Sarah Bove, James Collins,
Harry Glass, Annabel Holmes, Emma Jones, Lou Millward Tait
and Malcolm Tait

Think Publishing
The Pall Mall Deposit
124-128 Barlby Road, London W10 6BL
www.thinkpublishing.co.uk

ISBN 978-1-862057-91-3

2 4 6 8 10 9 7 5 3 1

Printed and bound by Millenium International Printing, China

www.anovabooks.com

INTRODUCTION

This is the book for anyone who has been bitten by the travel bug, seized by wanderlust or trotted the globe. If you are embarking on your own great odyssey or looking back fondly on your travelling days from your armchair this is a backpack buddy you can't be without.

It won't tell you anything about the nightlife in New Zealand, when the museums open in Moscow, or the best beds in Bogota. But it will keep you company wherever you are with amusing anecdotes, surprising snippets and treasured travel tips.

Even if your body can't wander, set your mind free to ponder some of the burning questions facing all travellers. Where exactly is the safest place to sit on an aeroplane? What is the strangest thing someone has stolen from a hotel room? Who mistook Hitler for a doorman? Why is an elephant struggling with the Euro? And where on earth is the world's largest peanut?

Whether you are waiting for a bus, whiling away the evening after some energetic sightseeing, or just trying to impress your fellow wayfarers with your travel trivia, *The Traveller's Pocket Companion* is for you. Enjoy the journey.

Rhiannon Guy, Editor

GIVE THE WORLD A BREAK

Avoid disturbing traditional festivities

Refrain from intruding on special occasions, especially if not accompanied by a guide who can act as an intermediary on your behalf.

Choose trains over planes

The fastest-growing contributors to global warming are planes. Trains are not only more environmentally friendly, they also provide a more interesting journey.

Responsible photography

Always ask people before taking their photos, respect their answer and keep your word if you promise to send them a copy. Do not use flash in places where it could damage delicate surfaces.

Local lingo

Try to learn several words in the local language to show your interest in the place and facilitate your welcome.

Respect the local dress code

When in Rome do as the Romans; respect the local clothing etiquette and forsake your bikini, tank tops or shorts when you are in a religious or traditional area.

FANTASTIC FESTIVITIES

The Bun Festival, Hong Kong, *May*

The Taoist Cheung Chau Bun Festival is one of Hong Kong's liveliest and most bizarre festivities. Every May for four days, huge bamboo towers are built and covered in buns. The festival used to involve people scaling the towers to retrieve the buns for good luck, but now people just turn up to look at the spectacular towering buns. On the third day of the festival, children are carried through the streets on poles and appear to float over the heads of the crowds. Other attractions include stilt walkers and people dressed as legendary characters.

BIG BANG

It's accepted that different countries have different customs. And it's perhaps fair to say that a cabbie in Scotland can expect a bit of light banter with passengers and possibly a small tip, especially if the passengers in question are newly-weds in good cheer. Jan Wawryluk was surprised, though, when just such a couple who he was driving to Edinburgh airport offered him a hand grenade for his troubles. Explanation? It was a relic from World War I, which they wouldn't be allowed to take on their flight.

After picking up a few more fares with this alarming antique in his cab, Mr Wawryluk decided to hand it in to police, who promptly called in the bomb disposal squad and sent a worldwide alert out to trace the couple who had given the explosive tip.

TRAVEL TEASERS

My first is in Ireland but never in Wales
My second's in engine but never in sails
My third is in Denmark but never in Greece
My fourth is in Paris and also in Nice
My fifth is in transport and also in fast
My whole is a nation that has a rich past
Answer on page 144

THE HITCHER

Abraham Lincoln always had a way with words. On one long walking journey, he hailed a stranger who was driving in his direction and asked if he would take his overcoat into town. The man agreed, but asked how Mr Lincoln expected to get it back: 'Oh, very easily,' came the reply, 'I intend to remain in it.'

G'DAY MATE

A trip down under turned from a sunny delight into a chilly fright for two teenagers from London in 2002. The pair had been looking forward to an antipodean adventure and had booked a holiday over the internet to Sydney, Australia. Or so they thought. They had actually booked a holiday to Sydney, Canada.

Apparently not noticing that all their fellow passengers were wrapped up against the impending chill, nor that they were flying over the Atlantic, it was not until the couple actually arrived in Nova Scotia that they realised the full extent of their mistake. Well, not quite: 'we thought we were stopping for a stopover' said Raeoul Sebastian.

The couple travelled back to the UK as soon as they could and presumably vowed to pay more attention to the country they were going to next time.

MESSAGE IN A BOTTLE

There are various ways of finding yourself a date these days, but if you really want to give yourself the best chance of finding Mr (or Mrs) Right, then there is no better method than scrawling a note, putting it in a plastic bottle and throwing it in the sea.

Or so thought Brenda Houston, a boat decorator, who threw this message from a cruise liner off southern Spain: 'I travel a lot on the sea. Tell me what you do in your life. Write to me.'

It took a few months, but eventually she got a bite. A fireman named Christian Jannussi found the bottle in the waters of the Méjean near his native Marseilles, and after three years of correspondence they fell in love.

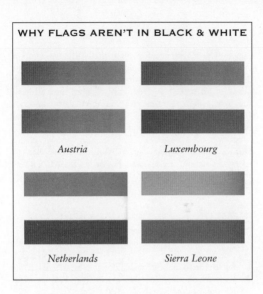

WHY FLAGS AREN'T IN BLACK & WHITE

Austria

Luxembourg

Netherlands

Sierra Leone

THE DESTINATION TOP 10

Country	International visitors (in 2004)
France	75,100,000
Spain	52,400,000
USA	46,100,000
China	41,800,000
Italy	37,100,000
UK	27,800,000
Mexico	20,600,000
Turkey	16,800,000
Germany	20,100,000
Russia	19,900,000

TOPSY TURVY GLOBE

So who was it who decided to put the North at the top of all the maps? And why? Step forward Ptolemy, famous 2nd-century Greek astronomer and a man very much ahead of his time. However, it wasn't until the 16th century when map-maker extraordinaire Mercator rediscovered that Ptolemy had placed North at the top of maps that North officially remained on top.

During the 1,300-year gap, religious interests dictated where the top of the globe was. For early Christians, it was the East, with Jerusalem in the centre of a flat circular map. This gave rise to the concept of the 'Orient'.

THE ISOLATION INDEX

		UN Isolation Index
1	**Easter Island,** South Pacific	149
2	**Rapa Iti,** South-west Pacific	130
3	**Kiritimati,** Line Islands, Central Pacific	129
4	**Jarvis Island,** Central Pacific	128
5=	**Kosrae,** Micronesia, Pacific	126
5=	**Malden,** Line Islands, Central Pacific	126
5=	**Starbuck,** Line Islands, Central Pacific	126
5=	**Vostok,** Line Islands, Central Pacific	126
9=	**Bouvet Island,** South Atlantic	125
9=	**Gough Island,** South Atlantic	125
9=	**Palmyra Island,** Central Pacific	125

The UN Isolation Index is calculated by adding together the square roots of the distances to the nearest island, group of islands and continent. For example, Easter Island is situated 2,000 miles from the nearest populated areas of Tahiti and Chile.

10

GRAND TOURING

If you'd been a nobleman in the 18th century you'd have completed (and in some cases perhaps started) your education with a period of travel around Europe known as a 'Grand Tour'. The length of your trip would depend on the size of your wallet, so anything from a few months to eight years was acceptable. The fashionable dots on the map you and your entourage had to try and join up were Venice, Naples, Sicily and Rome. You were also expected to return with a collection of bona fide classical antiquities to show off (a sort of Continental supermarket sweep), although many adventurers just returned with new, more virulent strains of venereal disease.

TAXI TRAVELLER LOSES HER WAY

The New World, full of the American dream, vast open spaces with breathtaking scenery and thriving cities. A must see on many a traveller's list. But how to get around? Plane, train or automobile? One women opted for automobile. But not just any car. Patricia Agness has no driving licence but she hates buses and planes. So, the only option seemed to be to get a cab. For 10,000 miles. The 55-yearold negotiated a one-dollar-a-mile fare and set off from her Florida home. Two drivers worked in eight hour shifts to try and complete the trip, which would take in 30 cities and finish in Alaska. However, the taxi drivers only made it to California before deciding they'd had enough. The sleep-deprived pair were replaced by a Californian cab driver after 2,500 miles and the journey went on. But not for that long. A commotion in a California hotel led to Agness being arrested and held for psychiatric tests: she had insisted on staying in the hotel's reception, rather than in a room.

LONGEST PLACE NAMES

Krung thep mahanakhon bovorn ratanakosin mahintharayutthaya mahadilok pop noparatratchathani burirom udomratchanivetmahasathan amornpiman avatarnsathit sakkathattiyavisnukarmprasit (167 letters)
This poetic name is usually abbreviated to 'Krung Thep', City of Angels, referring to Bangkok, Thailand's capital.

Taumatawhakatangihangakoauauotamateaturipukakapik imaungahoronukupokaiwhenuakitinatahu (85 letters)
'The place where Tamatea, the man with the big knees, who slid, climbed and swallowed mountains, known as land-eater, played on the flute to his loved one' is the Maori name of a hill in New Zealand.

Gorsafawddachaidraigddaneddogleddollonpenrhynareur draethceredigion (67 letters)
The Fairbourne Steam Railway in North Wales invented this name to rival their more famous Welsh counterpart below. It translates to 'The Mawddach station and its dragon teeth at the Northern Penrhyn Road on the golden beach of Cardigan Bay'.

Llanfairpwllgwyngyllgogerychwyrndrobwll-llantysiliogogogoch (58 letters)
This train station's official name 'St Mary's Church in the hollow of the white hazel near to the rapid whirlpool of the church of St Tysilio near the Red Cave' was said to be a prank, humorously thought up by a local tailor.

El Pueblo de Nuestra Senora la Reina de los Angeles de la Porciunucula (57 letters)
Who'd have thought 'The town of Our Lady the Queen of the Angels of the Little Portion' is the original name of Los Angeles, once the site of a Franciscan mission?

LANGUAGES OFFICIALLY SPOKEN
IN THE MOST COUNTRIES

		Number of countries
1	English	57
2	French	33
3	Arabic	23
4	Spanish	21
5	Portuguese	7
6=	Dutch	5
6=	German	5
8=	Chinese (Mandarin)	3
8=	Danish	3
8=	Italian	3
8=	Malay	3

ANOTHER SIDE TO THE COINS

When 12 countries switched to the Euro in 2002 it was hoped that, among other things, it would make life easier for tourists travelling between the countries. Perhaps it did.

But however many convergence tests were met by members, there remained one or two large problems when it came to monetary union. One of the most substantial lives in Lisbon Zoo and goes by the name of Jonas. Jonas is a five-tonne African bull elephant who once earned his keep accepting escudos from tourists, ringing a bell for them and hence being fed snacks. His livelihood was threatened when travellers began handing him strange coinage which didn't meet the simple criteria he had been taught: don't accept anything under 20 escudos. His keepers had to retrain him to keep him up with the times, possibly bringing into being the world's first crash course in elementary economics for elephants.

QUIZ HIGH-FLYERS

If you're bored and travelling through Singapore's Changi airport, don't fret, for you can take part in a Civil Aviation Authority daily quiz show. This 25-minute diversion, hosted by professional actors, runs 12 times a day and has so far attracted 4,000 game players and crowds of up to a 100 curious onlookers. It's time well spent as the winners get shopping vouchers that they can then spend in the airport before boarding their plane.

DISTINCTIVE DWELLINGS

Ice Hotel, Lapland, Sweden

The Ice Hotel in Lapland is forever changing. And make sure you're not there during a heat wave. This ice palace was first created in 1990, and every November a team of sculptors and architects lovingly re-crafts the large igloo hotel, complete with sparkling ballrooms, cinema, chapel and 'Absolut Ice Bar'. Every single bedroom is unique with all the furniture and fittings made from ice.

If you're not one for winter and hate the cold, don't worry: like the local Sami people, you'll sleep on a block of ice covered in cosy reindeer pelts.

A FIVE-STAR ORGY

They say any publicity is good publicity, but when the *People's Daily* in Zhuhai, China, reported an orgy at a five-star hotel involving 400 Japanese tourists and 500 prostitutes, that certainly wasn't the case. Although many would argue that the episode would have attracted more customers than it would lose, the authorities swiftly closed the hotel.

TRAVELLING CIRCUS

Large waterfalls constitute some of the most popular tourist attractions in the world, but some people are not content just to take a few snaps for their albums. Since 1901, 15 daredevils are thought to have gone over Niagara Falls (on the Canadian side) using barrels wrapped with inner tubes, kayaks and other contraptions, of which only 10 survived.

In 1960, a seven-year-old boy survived, wearing just an inflatable ring, when he went over as a result of a boating accident. And in 2003, Kirk Jones became the first man to survive the 180-ft drop without any device when he jumped in 'on impulse', although his mother later said the Falls had intrigued her son for years. He compared going over to 'being in a giant tunnel, going straight down, surrounded by water', which is hardly surprising: water goes over the Falls at a rate of 150,000 gallons to the second.

After his jump, Kirk faced a fine of around US$7,600, but was immediately hired as the 'world's greatest stunt man' by the touring Toby Tyler Circus.

FANTASTIC FESTIVITIES

Burial of the Sardine, Tenerife, Canary Islands, Spain, *February*

This annual festival takes place on Carnival Tuesday (usually the end of February) in several villages around the island. The festivities in Santa Cruz, for example, follow the slow-moving 'death' procession of a huge sardine (made from cloth) mounted on a throne. Its arrival, accompanied by men dressed as pregnant women and wailing widows, at the Plaza Europa is greeted by an enormous firework display with dancing in the street and the laying to rest of the celebrated sardine.

EAT ME

Quick, get a pen and paper! Early in 2004, *Zoo Weekly* ran a competition offering a jungle holiday with a tribe of cannibals. Interesting idea. The 'winner' would be whisked off (not up) to the Baliem Valley in Papua New Guinea to spend two weeks (if all went well) with the Korowai tribe, who sport tusks in their noses and piercings, wear nothing but long penis gourds... and eat people.

On the up side, the lucky person would be accompanied by a Mr Barker, who has known the tribe for years. On the downside, they would be travelling without maps or phones. But, Mr Barker was very reassuring on the subject: 'It should be OK. The really bad ones are the Korowai's neighbours, the Asmat, and they haven't eaten a Westerner for 40 years,' he said. Well, that's alright then.

Entrants had to write 25 words or less saying why they should go. Funnily enough only two words leap to mind.

OLD POSTER, NEW CAPTION

As he gazed out of the unmoving trolley, Josiah began to recollect some vague phrase involving the words 'cart', 'before' and 'horse'.

Ever waited a long time to catch a flight? Or sat for hours on the runway wondering whether the pilot is doing his duty-free shopping? Well, spare a thought for Merhan Karimi Nasseri. He has been waiting at Paris Charles de Gaulle for 10 years – but he's not waiting to check in, he's waiting to check out.

An Iranian exile expelled for his political beliefs, he was city hopping in Europe searching for relatives when a trap of bureaucracy snapped shut on him.

He had been awarded political asylum but in 1988 his refugee papers were stolen and he was returned from London to France where he arrived without a passport. The courts determined that he had entered the airport legally as a refugee and therefore could not be expelled from it, but the French government refused to allow him onto French soil and he has been in the airport ever since.

His clothes are clean, his moustache trimmed and his blazer hangs from an airport cart. Staff call him 'Alfred', and he reads a lot. He occasionally walks to the terminal doors, waits for them to open, and inhales the fresh air, but he never steps outside. He even gets his post sent there.

'He's a part of the airport', said the manager of one of the airport bars. A Lufthansa clerk added: 'That's his table, his chair, his place. He's one of us.'

ARSE!

If you want to attract tourists, you must learn how they think. When the company which ran the Peak Cavern in Derbyshire wanted to whip up more tourism to their caves following the Foot and Mouth crisis it renamed the site to its original title: Devil's Arse. The result?

A 30% increase in visitors.

FORMERLY KNOWN AS...

Belize – a country east of Guatemala in the Caribbean; formerly British Honduras

Benin – a country in western Africa; formerly Dahomey

Botswana – a country in south-central Africa; formerly Bechuanaland

Cambodia – a country in south-east Asia on the Gulf of Thailand; formerly Khmer Republic

Djibouti – a country in eastern Africa; formerly Afars and Issas

Ethiopia – a country in north-east Africa; formerly Abyssinia

Greece – a country in south-east Europe, with many islands; formerly Hellas

Lesotho – a country in southern Africa; formerly Basutoland

Malawi – a country in south-east Africa, east of Zambia; formerly Nyasaland

Nauru – an island country in the Pacific, south of the equator and west of Kiribati; formerly Pleasant Island

Sri Lanka – an island country in the Indian Ocean off south-east India; formerly Ceylon

Surinam – a country on the coast of South America; formerly Dutch Guiana

Taiwan – an island country off the south-east coast of China in the South China Sea; formerly Formosa

Thailand – a country in south-east Asia on the Gulf of Thailand; formerly Siam

Tuvalu – an island country in the western Pacific off Fiji; formerly Ellice Islands

United Arab Emirates – a country in eastern Arabia; formerly Trucial Oman

Vanuatu – an island country in the southern Pacific; formerly New Hebrides

Zimbabwe – a country in southern Africa; formerly Rhodesia

WHOM WAS THAT?

Enjoyment, relaxation and restlessness: these are just some of the reasons why we travel, but for Edward de Vere, the Earl of Oxford, his journey to the continent in the 1550s was prompted by a rather different motivation. The well-known wit, poet, patron of the theatre and favourite in the court of Queen Elizabeth, had 'accidentally let one off' when bowing low to her majesty. After seven years of embarrassment-fuelled journeying, he arrived home to be greeted by the Queen's words: 'Really my Lord, I had forgotten the fart'.

TAG TOTING

Most people collect postcards or stamps.
But not 14-year-old Raghav Somani from India.
He has the world's largest collection of airline luggage tags. In fact, he has amassed a total of 469 of them.
His collection includes tags made of leather and metal and even some special edition tags that were issued for the delegates of the 1992 US Republican convention by Continental Airlines.

DISTINCTIVE DWELLINGS

Madonna Inn, California, USA
Kitsch doesn't even cover this themed hotel. Over 40 years ago, when themed rooms were something of a novelty, the Madonna Inn decided to make every one of its 109 rooms unique. Some of the options include a cave room, a cabin room, a lace room and a leather room. But even if the interior isn't to your liking, the location will be: the rooms overlook the Pacific coast between San Francisco and Los Angeles.

Acapulco *2 measures white rum, ½ measure triple sec, ½ measure lime juice, 1 tsp sugar syrup, 1 egg white.* Shake the rum, triple sec, lime juice and sugar syrup over cracked ice. Add the egg white and shake. Serve in a chilled glass with a sprig of mint.

American Rose *1½ measures brandy, 1 tsp grenadine, ½ measure Pernod, half fresh peach (peeled), sparkling wine.* Blend the brandy, grenadine, Pernod and fresh peach together. Strain into a chilled glass, add sparkling wine and garnish with a peach slice.

Blue Hawaii *1½ measures white rum, ½ measure dark rum, ½ measure blue curacao, 3 measures pineapple juice, 1 measure coconut cream.* Shake the ingredients over cracked ice and serve in a chilled glass.

Cuba Libre *2 measures white rum, cola.* Half fill a glass with cracked ice. Pour over the rum and top up with cola. Stir gently to mix, add a splash of lime juice and decorate with a lime wedge.

French 75 *2 measures brandy, 1 measure lemon juice, 1 tsp sugar syrup, and chilled champagne.* Shake the brandy, lemon juice and sugar syrup over cracked ice. Top up with champagne and decorate with a twist of lemon.

Italian Margarita *1 measure amaretto, ½ measure cointreau, ½ measure tequila and 2 measures lime juice.* Blend ingredients with ice and serve in a salt-rimmed glass, garnish with a lime wedge.

Long Island Iced Tea *2 measures vodka, 1 measure gin, 1 measure tequila, 1 measure white rum, ½ measure triple sec, cola, a dash each of lemon and lime juice and sugar syrup.* Shake all the ingredients over cracked ice, reserving the cola to top up in a high-ball glass before serving. Decorate with a lemon or lime wedge.

Mexican Grasshopper
1 measure each of kahlua, white crème de caçao and cream. Shake over cracked ice and strain into a chilled cocktail flute.

Moscow Mule *2 measures vodka, 1 measure lime juice, ginger beer.* Shake the vodka and lime juice over cracked ice. Pour into a glass, top up with ginger beer and decorate with a wedge of lime.

Around the World *1 measure gin, 1 measure crème de menthe, 2 measures pineapple juice.* Shake the ingredients over cracked ice and serve in a chilled glass.

FAR AND AWAY

The 'remotest human settlement in the world' is the Edinburgh settlement on Tristan Da Cunha island in the southern Atlantic, which is able to sustain its 300 strong population thanks to its delicious crawfish and to collectors around the world who pay top dollar for its rare stamps.

The first settlers in the 1800s were from England; hence its native tongue is English. The island now boasts Americans, Europeans and South Africans, who share seven surnames amongst each other.

WORLD MUSIC

I Left My Heart in San Francisco – Tony Bennett
Copacabana – Barry Manilow
Vienna – Ultravox
New York, New York – Frank Sinatra
I Love Paris – Frank Sinatra
Barcelona – Freddie Mercury with Montserrat Caballe
One Night in Bangkok – Murray Head
Tulips from Amsterdam – Max Bygraves
On an Evening in Roma – Dean Martin

THE SIGNS AREN'T GOOD

Detour sign in Kyushu, Japan: Stop: Drive sideways.

From a Japanese information booklet about using a hotel air conditioner: Cooles and Heates: If you want just condition of warm in your room, please control yourself.

From a brochure of a car rental firm in Tokyo: When passenger of foot heave in sight, tootle the horn. Trumpet him melodiously at first, but if he still obstacles your passage then tootle him with vigour.

Two signs from a Majorcan shop entrance: English well talking. Here speeching American.

In a Hong Kong supermarket: For your convenience, we recommend courageous, efficient self-service.

In an Acapulco hotel: The manager has personally passed all the water served here.

Copenhagen airline: We take your bags and send them in all directions.

LIFE QUESTIONS...

It's the news many people have been longing to hear: being lazy is good for you. German professor Peter Axt believes that those who laze around in hammocks instead of exercising are more likely to live longer. So when you're lying on the beach, but feel you should be up and about, relax and top up your life account for a while.

But there's another side to this story: Siegfried Lehrl, from the University of Erlangen-Nuremberg, has declared that sunbathing and relaxation actually lowers your IQ. He has even quantified it: apparently two weeks of rest can dent the IQ by 20 points. But active travellers don't have to worry: it's boredom that's the intelligence killer.

GROUND CONTROL TO MAJOR TOM, DICK AND HARRY

On 28 April 2001, US multi-millionaire Dennis Tito became the world's first space tourist after paying US$20 million for a week's board and lodging on the International Space Station.

Mark Shuttleworth from South Africa went on the same extraterrestrial cruise in April the following year, and Lance Bass of the group N'Sync was planning on being the third, but the Russians stopped his training when he couldn't come up with the cash.

Now the race is on between private companies to tap into the market; after all, where better for a family holiday than space, where no-one can hear you scream?

A US$10 million 'X Prize' awaits the first private company to develop a reusable launch vehicle (RLV) capable of carrying the general public into space. The prize was set up in May 1996 to promote commercial human space flight and is a continuation of the early 20th century competitions that jump-started the aviation industry (Charles Lindbergh's grandson Eric is one of the prize's sponsors). There are 25 registered groups from seven countries currently competing.

It all comes down to money: it currently costs US$10,000 to get one pound (0.45kg) of passenger weight into the Earth's orbit. The new space planes will need to reduce this to US$1,000 per pound, if they are to bring the ticket within reach of even the biggest of the big spenders.

But, it is within sight: a 1998 NASA report suggests that improvements in technology could push fares as low as US$50,000, and possibly down to US$10,000 a decade later. And with a ticket price of US$50,000, there could be up to 500,000 passengers flying into space each year.

A LOAD OF HOT AIR

Archimedes worked out the principles of buoyancy more than 2,000 years ago, and may well have conceived of flying machines, but it was Joseph and Etienne de Montgolfier who invented the first hot-air balloon. The brothers were working in the family paper factory at Annonay, near Lyon in France, when they noticed that a shirt drying above the fire was rising and that scraps of paper in the fireplace flew up out of the chimney. They began experimenting with paper vessels elevated by hot air.

On 4 April 1783, their first unmanned balloon, made from fabric coated with alum and paper, flew for nearly two kilometres at a height of two metres. It was powered by burning straw,

manure and other materials in an attached fire pit. On 19 September, a sheep, a duck and a rooster became the first balloon passengers in another Montgolfier design; this time in the presence of King Louis XVI at Versailles. The balloon flew for eight minutes at a height of 500m before landing in the forests of Vaucresson three kilometres away. Whether the animals escaped or not is unclear.

Two months later, on 21 November, the Marquis François d'Arlandes and Jean Pilâtre de Rozier became the first humans to fly in an untethered balloon. They rose to 90m, waved their hats to the delighted crowds below, and then rose to 900m before touching back down.

GET YOUR COAT

The term 'erotodromomania' describes the abnormal impulse to travel to escape unwanted sexual situations, which perhaps explains the concept of gap years, or at least returning from them.

• The ancient Greek, Scylax of Carryanda, explored the Middle East in the 6th century BC. He was sent by the Emperor Darius of Persia who had ideas of conquering India.

• An ancient Egyptian, Hannu, made the first self-recorded exploring expedition. He sailed down the Red Sea and explored the southeastern areas of the Arabian peninsula around 2750 BC. He also went to Ethiopia and Somalia, returning to Egypt with souvenirs that included the spice myrrh before putting his story down in stone.

• Second-century BC Chinese explorer Zhang Quian travelled to the Steppes of central Asia during the Han Dynasty at a time when Emperor Han Wudi was looking to open trade relations with his distant neighbours. On his way to visit the Yueh-chih tribe, Quian was captured by the nomadic Hsiung-nu (the Huns) who imprisoned him for 10 years before he

managed to escape and continue the remaining 2,000 miles of his journey. His travels helped open up the beginnings of the famous Silk Road.

• Intrepid Eric the Red (the settler of Greenland) had an equally intrepid son, Leif Eriksson who is credited with being the first European to land on Newfoundland – around the year 1000 AD.

• St Brendan, also 'Brendan the Gold' and 'Brendan the Voyager' (484–c.578) was an Irish abbot, monastery founder and legendary sea voyager. He certainly sailed as far as the Hebrides and may even have got as far as the Canary Islands and the Azores.

• Marco Polo (1254–1324) famously crossed Asia to China to visit the Kublai Khan in Beijing. Polo's written accounts of his travels are the first Western record of coal, porcelain, gunpowder, printing, paper money and silk.

THE SIGNS AREN'T GOOD

In a Japanese hotel:
You are invited to take advantage of the chambermaid.

On the menu of a Polish hotel:
Salad a firm's own make; limpid red beet soup with
cheesy dumplings in the form of a finger; roasted
duck let loose; beef rashers beaten up in the country
people's fashion.

On the menu of a Swiss restaurant:
Our wines leave you nothing to hope for.

In an Austrian hotel catering to skiers:
Not to perambulate the corridors in the hours of repose
in the boots of ascension.

In a Bangkok dry-cleaner:
Drop your trousers here for best results.

Outside a Hong Kong tailor shop:
Ladies may have a fit upstairs.

**In the lobby of a Moscow hotel opposite a
Russian Orthodox monastery:**
You are welcome to visit the cemetery where famous
Russian and Soviet composers, artists, and writers are
buried daily except Thursday.

TRAVEL TEASERS

Where in the US:
M
TANA
Answer on page 144

DON'T WORRY, THEY SPEAK ENGLISH...

Percentage of English speakers

Barbados	100%	Jamaica	97%
Belize	65%	Liberia	96%
Bermuda	95%	Montserrat	100%
Granada	100%	Nigeria	50%
Guiana	75%	Papua New Guinea	66%

ST EDMUNDS, ETHIOPIA?

When travelling abroad, it's likely you'll find an English newspaper to read on the flight back, but how about a book about your own home town? Frank Warby was in Addis Ababa airport when he spotted a guidebook not of Europe nor Britain, but of Bury St Edmunds. The copy was 32 years old and included completely out-of-date pictures of the town and plans for a 'new' hospital which was actually completed in 1972.

WHO WEARS SHORT SHORTS?

Would not being able to wear a bikini influence your decision to book a trip? Apparently so, if Malaysia is your destination. Much to the dismay of its tourism minister Abdul Kadir Sheikh Fadzir and the tourism sector, the ban on bikinis has resulted in a severe drop in visitor numbers. But it's not just bikinis that are banned, the Muslim Opposition Party, ruling the state of Terengganu, has also segregated men and women at pools and hotels, and has prohibited unisex hair salons, karaoke outlets and pubs. The question is: do tourists have the right to act as they please, even if it is contrary to their host country's belief system and culture, or does a state have the right to impose restrictions on people's freedom?

MEET THE NEIGHBOURS

1. **China** (15 neighbours)
Afghanistan, Bhutan, India, Kazakhstan, Kyrgyzstan, Laos, Macau, Mongolia, Myanmar, Nepal, North Korea, Pakistan, Russia, Tajikistan, Vietnam

2. **Russia** (14 neighbours)
China, North Korea, Mongolia, Azerbaijan, Belarus, Estonia, Finland, Georgia, Kazakhstan, Latvia, Lithuania, Norway, Poland, Ukraine

3. **Brazil** (10 neighbours)
Argentina, Bolivia, Colombia, French Guiana, Guyana, Paraguay, Peru, Surinam, Uruguay, Venezuela

4= **Democratic Republic of the Congo** (9 neighbours)
Angola, Burundi, Central African Republic, Congo, Rwanda, Sudan, Tanzania, Uganda, Zambia

4= **Germany** (9 neighbours)
Austria, Belgium, Czech Republic, Denmark, France, Luxembourg, Netherlands, Poland, Switzerland

4= **Sudan** (9 neighbours)
Central African Republic, Chad, Democratic Republic of the Congo, Egypt, Eritrea, Ethiopia, Kenya, Libya, Uganda

7= **Austria** (8 neighbours)
Czech Republic, Germany, Hungary, Italy, Liechtenstein, Slovakia, Slovenia, Switzerland

7= **France** (8 neighbours)
Andorra, Belgium, Germany, Italy, Luxembourg, Monaco, Spain, Switzerland

7= **Turkey** (8 neighbours)
Armenia, Azerbaijan, Bulgaria, Georgia, Greece, Iran, Iraq, Syria

10= **Mali** (7 neighbours)
Algeria, Burkina Faso, Côte d'Ivoire, Guinea, Mauritania, Niger, Senegal

10= **Niger** (7 neighbours)
Algeria, Benin, Burkina Faso, Chad, Libya, Mali, Nigeria

10= **Saudi Arabia** (7 neighbours) Iraq, Jordan, Kuwait, Oman, Qatar, UAE, Yemen

10= **Tanzania** (7 neighbours) Burundi, Kenya, Malawi, Mozambique, Rwanda, Uganda, Zambia

10= **Ukraine** (7 neighbours) Belarus, Hungary, Moldova, Poland, Romania, Russia, Slovakia

10= **Zambia** (7 neighbours) Angola, Democratic Republic of the Congo, Malawi, Mozambique, Namibia, Tanzania, Zimbabwe

The largest landlocked country is Kazakhstan (1,049,156 square miles). Its neighbours are China, Kyrgyzstan, Turkmenistan, Russia and Uzbekistan.

A NO FRILLS COCK-UP

People tend to return from travelling with horror stories of delays, lost passports and hotel mix-ups, but just occasionally, it does work the other way. The Dryer family from Liverpool spotted flights to Florida for £15 each – that's £485 cheaper than they should have been. The family of six enjoyed their trip to Disney World for the grand total of £90, making an even grander saving of £2,910. The travel company blamed one of its website staff, although there were sightings of a large clothed mouse in the company buildings at that time.

ESCAPE TO PYRRHIC VICTORY

We've all heard epic escape stories of determined and desperate people crossing whole countries, even continents, in order to return home safely. But there are others, which in contrast, seem rather pathetic. Ronald Thomas was serving a 12-year burglary sentence at a state prison in Oklahoma when he managed to escape, steal a prison van and make his getaway. He drove 150 miles north to Kansas before phoning the police to say that he was lost, and could he go back to jail please. Oh dear.

GIVE THE WORLD A BREAK

Preserve coral reefs As a result of tourism and pollutants, 27% of coral reefs, the most biodiverse of marine ecosystems, have been destroyed. Be a responsible tourist and refrain from touching, anchoring on or retrieving pieces of coral reefs.

Don't stand out To avoid attracting thieves and cultural segregation, be discrete and don't flash expensive personal belongings.

Misconceptions of time Time is relative, so relax; don't count on other cultures to be punctual as they often do not share our fixed, mathematical notion of time.

Verify policy statements Enquire about your tour operator's responsible-tourism policies, such as local and fair employment schemes, and report any discrepancies you have encountered to tourism authorities.

Avoid golfing holidays Golfing holidays are very damaging to local communities and the environment. On average, one golf course necessitates 1,500kg of pesticides per year, and can consume as much water as 60,000 villagers.

THE WHO'S WHO OF THE QE2

• The cruise liner Queen Elizabeth 2 moves six inches for each gallon of diesel she burns.

• The ship should always be written QE2 rather than QEII, which is the actual queen (if you bragged about a ride to America on the QEII you might eventually find yourself in prison).

• If preparing a speech about such a voyage, never write about chatting to QEII in a queue about 'who's who' on the QE2, for you are steering yourself into choppy waters.

CHEAP HIT

It seems there is a new drug around. It's not class 'A', it's not even class 'B'. In fact, it's what's known as 'getting from A to B'. Too much of anything can be detrimental they say (damn them) and with the advent of low-cost airlines and cheap flights, it seems there is a wave of addicts who just can't get enough of the amazing deals on offer.

A recent survey found that 46% of 18 to 35 year olds have skipped work to take advantage of a cut-price break, 20% have also admitted to missing a family wedding, 36% have missed a date and 37% have missed a friend's birthday. Symptoms of this 'jet pack' are square eyes and twitchy fingers, the result of hours spent mouse-clicking on the internet for the best deals. You will find many of these poor souls in London, where a fifth of this age group survive on at least three such holidays a year.

FREE AS A BIRD

You're on a jumbo jet, you've taken off and are cruising at a reasonable altitude when the captain announces: 'Ladies and gentlemen, it's now safe to undo your seatbelts, your trousers, shirts, skirts...'

Yes, the good old US of A have organised the world's first flight for passengers wanting to fly *au naturel* (though they should really use hang-gliders for a more realistic experience).

The flight, from Miami to Mexico, required passengers to be clothed for check-in and take off, but once they were thousands of feet in the air, it was acceptable for them to disrobe. That's one flight on which you surely would want to know who you were sitting next to.

There was only one extra rule: sex was surely not permitted during the flight. No, that would be taking it all just too far.

Blackbeard may have been a pirate, but he insisted that gentlemen should be able to walk the plank with dignity.

TRAVEL TEASERS

Fill in the blanks twice to make two different explorers.
M***O P***

Answer on page 144

THE WORLD'S LEADING
AND LAGGING AIRLINES

	First Class	Business	Premium Economy
Aeroflot	55	38	32
Air Zimbabwe	43		30
Qantas	78	50	31
Cathay Pacific	79	60	32
British Airways	78	73	38	31

The number is the distance, in inches, between the back of one row of seats and the back of the row of seats in front.

TRAVELLING IN DISGUISE

René-Auguste Caillié (1799–1838) was the first European to visit Timbuktu and return. Born to poor French peasants, he was obsessed with the idea of seeing the city, renowned as the African El Dorado. Timbuktu, founded by nomads in the 12th century, rapidly became a major trading post for the caravans of the Sahara Desert, as well as a rich Islamic cultural centre. It gained almost mythical status as a city of gold where Europeans were not welcome. Caillié studied Arabic and the Islamic religion during his 11 years of preparation. In April 1827, he left the coast of West Africa on his expedition, reaching Timbuktu a year later, despite being ill for five months. In order to enter the desert city, he disguised himself as an Arab trader, much to the chagrin of European explorers of the time. Disillusioned with Timbuktu, which had 'become simply a salt trading outpost filled with mud-walled homes in the middle of a barren desert', he left after two weeks and returned home to France. Caillié published three volumes about his travels and was awarded a 10,000-Franc prize from the Geographical Society of Paris.

LARGEST COUNTRIES NAMED
AFTER PEOPLE

1. United States of America
Named after: Amerigo
Vespucci (Italy; 1451–1512)
3,539,245 square miles

2. Saudi Arabia
Named after: Abdul Aziz
ibn-Saud (Nejd; 1882–1953)
830,000 square miles

3. Bolivia
Named after: Simon Bolivar
(Venezuela; 1783–1830)
418,685 square miles

4. Colombia
Named after: Christopher
Columbus (Italy; 1451–
1506) *401,044 square miles*

5. Philippines
Named after: Philipp II
(Spain; 1527–1506)
115,124 square miles

6. Falkland Islands
Named after: Lucius Cary,
2nd Viscount Falkland

(UK; 1610–1643)
4,700 square miles

7. Northern Mariana
Named after: Maria Teresa
(Austria; 1717–1780)
184 square miles

8. Wallis and Futuna
Named after: Samuel
Wallis (UK; 1728–1795)
105 square miles

9. Cook Islands
Named after: Captain
James Cook (UK; 1728–
1779) *93 square miles*

10. Marshall Islands
Named after: Captain John
Marshall (UK; 1748–
c.1818) *70 square miles*

*It is debated whether
China was named after
the Emperor Chin…
If so, it would obviously
rank first.*

TRAVEL TEASERS

Two twins are born 20 minutes apart on a boat.
The following year, the younger twin celebrates her
birthday. Two days later, her older twin brother
celebrates his. How is this possible?
Answer on page 144

FANTASTIC FESTIVITIES

Montana Testicle Festival,
Clinton, Montana, USA
September
Includes live music, the
'Testy Festy Awards', bull-
shit bingo, body painting, a
wet teeshirt competition, a
hairy chest contest, loads
to drink and of course –
tasting some testes. The
health conscious needn't
worry though: 'they're
70% or more protein and
boneless. Oh, and they
belong to bulls too.'

**World Championship
Cardboard Boat Race,**
Heber Springs, Arkansas,
USA *July*
Leave it to Bill Clinton's
home state to perfect the
art of keeping a cardboard
boat afloat. The homemade
boats are fashioned from
cardboard, duct tape, glue
and paint before the race
on Greers Ferry Lake.

**US International Jousting
Competition,** Estes Park,
Colorado, USA *September*
International Jousting
Competition held at the
Longs Peak Scottish/Irish
Highland Festival in Estes
Park, Colorado. Some
50,000 people show up to
not only witness jousting,
but also ring spearing,
spear throwing and shield
hitting.

**Deniliquin Play on the
Plains and World Record
Ute Muster,** Deniliquin,
NSW, Australia
September/October
A world record bid is held
each year on the plains to
muster the largest parade
of legally-registered utes in
the world.

**Broomstick Beating
Festival,** Mamala and
Morella, Indonesia *January*
A week after the end of
Ramadan the men of these
two villages find the time
and inclination to beat
each other's bare backs
with broomsticks. Once the
sticks are down, they apply
'mamala oil' made from
coconuts to their wounds,
apparently giving them
supernatural powers.
Changing clothes in a
phone booth seems tame in
comparison. Accept no
substitute.

35

DON'T LEAVE ME HIGH

The highest airport in the world is Bangda in Tibet, at 4,300m (14,100ft). That makes it a little less reassuring to hear the pilot say: 'We are now cruising at 15,000ft'. You'll be pleased to hear, it also has one of the longest runways at 5,500m (18,000ft), presumably to give planes time to take off in the thin Himalayan air.

The two lowest airports in the world both have a rather morbid ring to them. First, there's Furnace Creek Airport in Death Valley National Park, which sits 64m (210ft) below sea level. And, if you really want to limbo in to land, there's Israel's I Bar Yehuda airport near the Dead Sea, which hides away at a shy but incredible 386m (1,266ft) below sea level.

And if you're thinking, you'll never visit airports like these, Amsterdam's Schiphol International Airport is a little deeper than 6ft under – it stands at 3m (11ft) below sea level.

DISTINCTIVE DWELLINGS

Underwater hideaway, Florida, USA

For a splashing good time, spend a night at Jules' Undersea Lodge, allegedly the first and only underwater hotel. The watery retreat was previously a research laboratory but opened in 1986 as a luxury retreat for divers. The only way to reach the hotel is by scuba diving since it is five fathoms under the surface of a mangrove lagoon. But don't worry if you're not up on your scuba, a three-hour class will qualify inexperienced guests to make the trip.

After arriving in the underwater world, guest can enjoy unlimited dive trips and a gourmet dinner and breakfast prepared by the lodge's very own mer-chef. Might fish be on the menu, per chance?

SPANISH LIES

On reaching the Yucatan in 1517, invading Spaniard Francisco Fernandez de Cordoba asked the Mayan natives what they called the region; they answered 'Yucatan' which meant, in their language, 'I don't understand you'. Cordoba wasn't the first European to land in this area. A previous expedition of 1511 had been shipwrecked on the coast and the sailors were taken prisoner, bringing European disease (probably smallpox) to the Mayans which decimated their numbers in waves over the next five years. Cordoba was not only looking for conquest, but for slaves to replace the native Cuban population who were already being killed off by European disease and slavery. On landing in the Yucatan, he found a people of sophisticated architects and artisans with whom he traded for gold artifacts before eventually conquering the whole area.

FOREIGN PARTS

If you die in Spain or Greece some of your organs may be removed for post mortem purposes – and if they are, they might be retained and not necessarily re-united with your body before repatriation.

A MAN FOR ALL REASONS

St Christopher is not only the patron saint of travellers, he can also be called upon by:
Car drivers • Taxi drivers • Bachelors • Brunswick, Germany • Boatmen • Bookbinders • Bus drivers • Fruit dealers • Gardeners • St Kitts
The good fellow can also be relied upon for protection against lightning, pestilential archers, floods, hailstorms and toothache.

WHAT TYPE OF TRAVELLER ARE YOU?

In 2002, the Travel Industry Association of America prepared a report on the inclinations of western tourists and their attitudes towards environmental issues. They came up with the definition of 'geotourism', which can be described as: 'tourism that sustains or enhances the geographical character of the place being visited – its environment, culture, aesthetics, heritage and the well-being of its residents'.

The following types of traveller were determined from the survey. Which one are you?

Geo-Savvys
- 43 years average age
- 41% have kids in household
- 74% work full/part-time
- 12% are retired
- 44% travelled internationally in past three years
- 83% visit destinations with authentic historic and archaeological sites
- 81% prefer small-scale accommodations run by local people
- 81% travel to experience people, lifestyles and cultures very different from their own
- 80% visit small towns and rural areas
- 73% feel it is important to learn about their destination's people, history, and culture

Urban Sophisticates
- 45 years average age
- 30% have kids in household
- 73% work full/part-time
- 12% are retired
- 73% are past-year air travellers
- 73% prefer destinations offering authentic historic or archaeological sites
- 86% take trips where they can explore historic and charming towns and locations
- 74% prefer destinations that offer a wide variety of cultural/arts events and attractions
- 63% also enjoy visiting large cities, as well as high quality accommodations with excellent facilities and fine dining

Good Citizens

- 55 years average age
- 28% have kids in household
- 54% work full/part-time
- 34% are retired
- 38% travelled internationally in past three years
- 88% want high levels of cleanliness
- 79% want high levels of safety and security
- 60% want high quality services and personnel
- 43% want to meet other travellers who share their interests

Traditionals

- 58 years average age
- 24% have kids in household
- 43% work full/part-time
- 42% are retired
- 65% seek no surprises when they travel
- 77% prefer family-friendly destinations
- 66% prefer trips to places where their families were from
- 53% prefer groups tours with pre-set itineraries and tour guides
- 45% want to meet other travellers who share their interests

Wishful Thinkers

- 32 years average age
- 50% have kids in household
- 81% work full/part-time
- 3% are retired
- 24% travelled internationally in past three years
- 48% like outdoor adventure, risk and excitement
- 46% like to travel to remote locales
- 35% like primitive travel in the wilderness
- 54% like trips to large cities
- 54% want high quality accommodations, excellent facilities and fine dining
- 45% want luxury and pampering

Apathetics

- 46 years average age
- 42% have kids in household
- 67% work full/part-time
- 17% are retired
- 18% travelled internationally in past three years
- 89% want high levels of cleanliness
- 65% want no surprises
- 62% want many forms of entertainment
- 51% don't eat unfamiliar foods when travelling

AKA

Nicknames for some American cities

Boston, MA	*Beantown*
San Francisco, CA	*Golden Gate City*
Savannah, GA	*Garden City*
New Orleans, LA	*Crescent City*
Los Angeles, CA	*City of Angels*
Philadelphia, PA	*City of Brotherly Love*
New York City, NY	*Big Apple*
Dayton, OH	*Birthplace of Aviation*
Chicago, IL	*Second City*
International Fall, MN	*Icebox of the US*
Denver, CO	*Mile-high City*
Pittsburgh, PA	*Iron City*
Detroit, MI	*Motown*
Nashville, TN	*Music City*
Akron, OH	*Rubber City*
Hollywood, CA	*Tinseltown*
Portland, OR	*Rose City*
Indianapolis, IN	*Monument City*

AHOY THERE

There's low self esteem, and then there's low self a'steam... Inspired by Dorian Gray's words ('Live the wonderful life that is in you. Be afraid of nothing'), US adventurer Richard Halliburton paid the lowest ever toll to cross the Panama Canal when he swam it in 1928. The authorities had told him that the locks would only be filled for a ship, so he declared himself the SS *Halliburton* and was granted passage through. Like all other vessels, his toll was assessed by his tonnage; he weighed 140lb, and so paid 36 cents. It's a wonder there are not more HMS *Backpackers* to be found these days.

THE SIGNS AREN'T GOOD

In a Czechoslovakian tourist agency:
Take one of our horse-driven city tours – we guarantee no miscarriages.

In a Rhodes tailor shop:
Order your summers suit. Because is big rush we will execute customers in strict rotation.

A German sign:
It is strictly forbidden on our Black Forest camping site that people of different sex, for instance, men and women, live together in one tent unless they are married with each other for that purpose.

In a Zurich hotel:
Because of the impropriety of entertaining guests of the opposite sex in the bedroom, it is suggested that the lobby be used for this purpose.

In an advertisement by a Hong Kong dentist:
Teeth extracted by the latest Methodists.

In a Rome laundry:
Ladies, leave your clothes here and spend the afternoon having a good time.

MOST EXPENSIVE COUNTRIES IN WHICH TO BUY A BIG MAC

1	Iceland	US$7.44
2	Norway	US$6.63
3	Switzerland	US$5.05
4	Denmark	US$4.84
5	Sweden	US$4.59
6	UK	US$3.90
7 =	USA	US$3.22
7 =	Turkey	US$3.22
8	New Zealand	US$3.16
9 =	South Korea	US$3.08
9 =	Canada	US$3.08

OLD POSTER, NEW CAPTION

'Ah, no, Mr President,' said the helpful aide, 'the pretty boat goes over here, in the big water.'

BRITISH CONSULATES CAN...

...issue emergency passports

...contact relatives to ask them to help a traveller in distress

...help find local lawyers, interpreters and doctors

...arrange for a next of kin to be informed about death and advise on procedures

...visit you if you're arrested or in prison and arrange for messages to be sent to relatives or friends

...put you in touch with organisations who help trace missing persons

...speak to local authorities on your behalf

Only as a last resort will they lend you money to get you home.

SURVIVAL TIPS

Water

• In a disaster situation a good cup of tea restores morale. Tea quenches thirst; coffee exacerbates it.

• Finding water in a survival situation must be the first priority.

• Be suspicious of any pool with no green vegetation growing around it or with bones lying around the side.

• Always boil water from wild pools or rivers.

• The average person loses about five pints of water a day. Fluid loss can be reduced by: avoiding exertion; not smoking, staying in the shade; eating as little as possible (digestion draws water from the vital organs into the digestive tract); never drinking alcohol when water is scarce; trying not to talk; wearing clothes to prevent excess water loss by sweat drying on the skin.

• After a long period of dehydration, you will vomit if you gulp water too fast, so take small sips at first.

• Never drink urine or sea water because of the high salt content which will cause further dehydration.

• If desperate, animal eyes, including salt water fish, are a good source of pure water.

FANTASTIC FESTIVITIES

St John's Pig Parade, Balayan, Philippines, *June*
To celebrate San Juan Bautista (John the Baptist), every June the people of Balayan put together a parade. But it's not just any parade: dozens of fully clothed roast suckling pigs are carried through the town on litters, sitting up on little chairs. The baptism of St John is re-enacted in the festival, which includes a lot of water. So don't be surprised when a huge water fights break out and unsuspecting passers-by become the target for a good dousing.

FLYING LANDMARKS

17 December, 1903
Orville and Wilbur Wright's Wright Flyer made the first successful flight by a powered, heavier-than-air machine. Orville piloted the first flight – which lasted 12 seconds and covered 120ft.

21 May, 1927
Charles A Lindbergh completed the first solo nonstop transatlantic flight in history. The Spirit of St Louis made the 3,610-mile flight from Long Island, New York, to Paris, France, in 33 hours, 30 minutes.

14 October, 1947
A Bell X-1 – named 'Glamorous Glennis' by its pilot, US Air Force Captain Charles E 'Chuck' Yeager – became the first plane to fly faster than the speed of sound, reaching a speed of 700 miles per hour at an altitude of 43,000ft.

10 January, 1980
David J Springbett completed the fastest around the world flight using scheduled aircraft in 44 hours, six minutes.

23 April, 1984
Kanellos Kanellopoulos made the longest-ever flight in a human-powered aircraft, travelling 71 miles.

20 November, 1984
Pilot Julian RP Nott and crewman Spider Anderson set a world altitude record for a pressurised balloon, flying to 17,766ft.

16 August, 1995
Concorde completed the fastest around-the-world flight by a commercial jet in 31 hours, 27 minutes and 49 seconds.

1 March, 1999
The first successful nonstop flight around the world in a balloon. Bertrand Piccard and Brian Jones made the 28,431-mile journey from Château d'Oex in the Swiss Alps to the Egyptian desert in 19 days, 21 hours, and 55 minutes.

OLD POSTER, NEW CAPTION

'No, *you* fool', groaned Stephenson.
'Not *that* type of rocket!'

SIGNS YOU FLY TOO MUCH

• You have a favourite trolley at the airport.
• You can mime along with the safety announcement.
• As far as you're concerned, more than five peanuts
at a time is just plain indulgent.
• Jet lag is your normal state.
• You think drinks only come in single serving
sized bottles and cans.
• You are surprised that at the cinema you don't
have to use headphones or crane your neck 45 degrees
to see the screen.
• You are continually amazed when there is no queue
for the bathroom when you are at home.
• You find metal cutlery too heavy and are unnerved
when it takes less than 20 minutes to saw through
a piece of meat.
• You know the duty-free catalogue off by heart.
• You have enough mini tubes of toothpaste to last
you a lifetime

GIVE THE WORLD A BREAK

Shop and eat locally
Avoid all-inclusive tour packages that leach up to 80% of tourist profits, so your spending can directly benefit the locals.

Do your research in advance
Knowing the customs and the politico-social frame of the country in addition to the places to visit beforehand will deepen a visitor's appreciation of and interaction with the locals and their environment.

Use public transport
Rather than renting a car, public transport is the best way to diminish your environmental footprint and meet people.

The grass is not always greener on the other side
Concentrate on the beautiful assets your nearby area has to offer to reduce long-distance travel.

Give respectfully
Offering useful gifts such as school materials, donations or staple foods through established structures of authority, usually a village chief or head of family, is the most effective way to show your appreciation.

STRANGE WEE BEASTIE

Love it or hate it, trophy hunting was often a part of travelling for gentlemen in the past, bringing a sense of adventure, danger to their trips and prestige upon themselves. Hunting tigers in India, big game hunting in Africa, perhaps an epic struggle with a marlin out in the open ocean... and what about a Hemingwayesque battle with a fierce, wild haggis in Scotland? A third of American tourists believe a haggis is a real animal, and almost a quarter arrive in Scotland hoping to hunt one down. A haggis on the wall next to the stag's head would complete an impressive collection.

BECKS AND BEATRIX

Fascinating culture, stunning scenery, delicious cuisine: there are many reasons why we choose the holiday destinations we do. So you might expect the same from those visiting our shores. Perhaps visitors want to see for themselves the architecture of Buckingham Palace and Westminster Abbey, or perhaps they want to take in the rolling English hills or taste fish and chips while sitting by the English seaside. But then again, maybe not. It seems the Japanese come for some completely different reasons.

Following the popularity of the England captain in Japan during the 2002 World Cup, the Japan Travel Bureau offered 'Beckham tours' to his birthplace in East London, his school in East Chingford and Old Trafford. Presumably followed by a hop across to LA. That's 14 hours and 6,000 odd miles to travel to see a footballer's house. Pretty crazy, huh? Then again perhaps not. According to the Japan Travel Bureau, the second most popular attraction for Japanese tourists is none other than an imaginary bunny rabbit, whose creator has been dead for over 60 years. Peter Rabbit more popular than Big Ben? Who'd have thought it?

NEW WORLDS

Travelling has always represented new horizons, not least for the millions of people who emigrated to America with the hope of starting a better life for themselves and their families. Charlie Chaplin was discovered by producer Mack Sennett while he was travelling with a British troupe touring America in 1913. Sennett signed him for US$150 a week, and within just seven years he had appeared in 69 films and was earning US$10,000 a week.

WHAT'S IN A NAME?

Prince Edward Island,
Canada
Renamed in honour of
Edward, Duke of Kent
(father of Queen Victoria)
in 1799

Tasmania, Australia
Named after Dutch naviga-
tor Abel Tasman who first
sighted it in 1642

The Cook Islands,
New Zealand
Named after English sea
captain James Cook who
explored them in 1773
and 1777

Williamsburg,
Virginia, USA
Named after King William
of Orange during his reign

Athens, Greece
Named after Athena,
goddess of wisdom and
knowledge

Victoria Falls,
Zimbabwe, Zambia
Explorer David Livingstone
named them after Queen
Victoria in 1855

Cody, Wyoming,
The Rocky Mountain
States, USA
Named after Buffalo Bill
Cody in 1896 when its
founder, a real- estate spec-
ulator, wanted to use
it to attract settlers

Bermuda
Named after the sea
captain Juan de Bermudez,
who first sited the islands
somewhere around 1503

Jaipur, India
Named after the warrior
and astronomer Maharaja
Jai Singh II who lived from
1693 to 1743 – he planned
and founded the famous
pink city

TRAVEL TEASERS

Unscramble the following to make a country:
LAFND
Answer on page 144

BOXED

Some people will do anything to get where they want to go without paying, not least dodging a train or a bus fare by hiding in the toilet. But to avoid paying a US$320 plane ticket, you need to take it to the next level.

Twenty-five year old Charles D McKinley, a 5ft 9in shipping clerk from Brooklyn, New York, climbed inside a shipping crate 3ft wide and 3ft deep (and you thought economy class was cramped) and airmailed himself to Texas to see his folks. He would have gotten away with it had he not popped up on arrival to shake the delivery driver's hand. He was reported and charged as a stowaway, a federal misdemeanour.

DISTINCTIVE DWELLINGS

Salt Palace and Spa Hotel, Salar de Uyuni, Bolivia. The weary traveller, wandering on the prehistoric and surreal salt flats 12,500ft up in the south-west of Bolivia, will no doubt think he has been there slightly too long when he sees this hotel made almost entirely out of sodium carbonate (for want of a livelier euphemism). The roof, walls, bar, tables and chairs, even the beds (will this please the weary traveller?) are all made of salt.

The hotel was built in 1993 by Juan Quesada, who saw the salt, saw the tourists that flocked to the site (it's one of Bolivia's main attractions), and brought them together in this 'first' for the hotel and catering industry. Twelve guest rooms with 24 beds and shared bathrooms surround a central courtyard. Rather like ice, salt makes for good building blocks. The sun heats it in the day and at night, when temperatures drop below freezing outside, the guests remain snug within. Apparently there's a notice asking customers not to lick the walls so the place doesn't disappear.

THE SIGNS AREN'T GOOD

Advertisement for donkey rides in Thailand:
Would you like to ride on your own ass?

In a Swiss mountain inn:
Special today – no ice cream.

Notice outside a Paris dress shop:
Dresses are for street walking.

In a Bangkok temple:
It is forbidden to enter a woman even a foreigner if dressed as a man.

In a Tokyo bar:
Special cocktails for the ladies with nuts.

In a Moscow hotel room:
If this is your first visit to the USSR, you are welcome to it.

In the office of a Roman doctor:
Specialist in women and other diseases.

BEACH BOMBS

When we travel to countries with warmer climes we may realistically worry about certain things. We might be afraid of snakes, or scorpions. We might be afraid to go in the water, fearful of what is lurking in the depths.

But we should actually be more afraid of sitting in the shade: falling coconuts kill around 150 people every year, 10 times more than those killed by sharks.

British travel insurance company Club Direct now provides insurance against these lethal beach bombs, which, on their short journey south from the branch, reach speeds of 50 miles an hour and can land on a person with a force greater than one tonne. Ow.

The subject was looked into in detail by one Professor Peter Barss, of McGill University in Montreal, who won the 2001 IG Nobel Prize for Medicine (Awarding Institution: the Annals of Improbable Research) for his paper 'Injuries due to falling coconuts'.

WORLD FIRSTS

1st motorway: the German autobahn opened May 1921
1st UK motorway: the M1, opened in 1959; the first
section was 72 miles long and cost £50 million to build
1st UK train buffet car: on the LMS train service from
Euston to Nottingham in 1932
1st fare-paying passenger flight in the UK: from
Brooklands to Hendon in 1911
1st motorised coach tour: the six-day continental excursion from Paris to Aix-les-Bains in 1898
1st duty-free shop: opened in Shannon airport in 1947;
at first, it stocked neither tobacco nor alcohol

TRAVELLING IN DISGUISE

Charles II (1630-1685) was intelligent, religiously tolerant
and a patron of scientific research and the arts, but somewhat lazy as a ruler, and a hedonistic character. His era is
remembered as the time of 'Merry Olde England'. He was
forced into exile after the English Civil War. He wandered
in disguise in his kingdom for six weeks until he engineered
a passage to France, through the isles of Scilly and Jersey.
In 1651, he was proclaimed King of Scotland. He returned
and invaded England, but was defeated by Cromwell's
army. Charles once again fled to France, where he lived a
poor existence. He roamed around Germany and the
Spanish Netherlands for several years before being invited
back to England as the Commonwealth dissolved in 1660.
The monarchy, although limited in scope by the strong parliament, was successfully restored. The Tory and Whig
Parties were formed during those interregnum years.
Charles's reign saw an appalling plague in 1665 and the
Great Fire of London in 1666. In 1681, Charles dissolved
Parliament for the last time. From henceforth he ruled as
an absolute monarch.

SURVIVAL TIPS

Cold

• Avoid walking on icebergs as they can turn over without warning.

• Should you ever kill a polar bear or seal, don't eat their livers as they contain toxic quantities of vitamin A.

• Avoid falling into ice-cold water. Exposed parts will freeze in about four minutes, you will be unconsciousness in seven minutes and death will occur in 15 minutes.

• In cold climates, cold wind can freeze unprotected flesh in minutes.

• Wool is best for inner garments: cotton absorbs moisture and if you're wearing wet cotton, you can lose heat 240 times faster than when the cotton is dry. If necessary remove cotton clothes and dry them individually.

• To avoid frostbite, contract and relax your face to stop stiff patches forming and to exercise muscles. Keep hands moving too or your fingers will freeze and fall off. The first signs of frostbite are waxy, blackened or reddening skin. Ears, nose and fingers are most at risk.

• Tight clothing reduces circulation and quickens frostbite.

• Get rid of any snow on the body before taking shelter; it will turn to water, dampen clothing and reduce temperature.

• Keep gloves on and keep them dry.

• Spilt petrol will freeze flesh instantly and cause frostbite far quicker than water.

• Tiredness increases the risk of frostbite so rest is important.

• Avoid camping in hollows as this is where frost collects.

HANDY HOWDIES

Japanese	*Konnichi wa*
Macedonian	*Zdravo*
Nepali	*Namaste*
Norwegian	*Nei*
Portuguese	*Ola*
Russian	*Privet*
Swahili	*Jambo*
Thai	*Sawat dii*
Welsh	*Dydd da*

LEFT OR RIGHT?

In 1998, a Roman quarry was discovered at Blunsdon Ridge near Swindon with an access road leading to the rock face. There were two sets of cart tracks: the one on the left, facing the quarry wall, was shallow, while the departing tracks, on the right, were deep from the weight. We can therefore conclude that the Romans drove on the left-hand side in Britain.

Roman coins have also been found depicting horse riders passing one another right shoulder to right shoulder. This is further proof of keeping to the left in ancient times.

WHICH HAT?

When entering a temple or a shrine, or even if you're just braving the elements, a well-prepared traveller should always have a hat on standby. A strong canvas hat with a wide brim is good for all weathers, but will need some kind of tie to stop it flying off in strong winds. If you buy it slightly too big, you can line the top with a handkerchief to make it warmer. Line the band with the same handkerchief to act as a sweatband when the weather's hot.

WHY DO THE BRAZILIANS
SPEAK PORTUGUESE?

Four years before Christopher Columbus landed on what he thought was Japan, Bartolomeu Dias reached the southernmost tip of Africa. The powerful rulers of Spain and Portugal thus turned to the Pope to help set up Christian rule in the newfound territories.

In 1455, Pope Calixtus III divided the world between Spain and Portugal, giving one the north and the other the south of the Canary Islands. But this didn't seem fair. With the untold riches that potentially existed below the equator and the New World of the Americas holding much promise, Pope Alexander VI Borgia redivided the world between Spain and Portugal according to a meridian stretching from Pole to Pole 100 leagues to the west of Cape Verde. On 7 June 1494, the Treaty of Tordesillas moved the boundary 270 leagues west. And this is why Portuguese is spoken in Brazil, and Spanish is spoken throughout the rest of South America.

BIG GIRL

One of New York's most famous monuments, the Statue of Liberty is not actually American. It was constructed in France in 1875 and was presented to the US on its completion on 4 July 1884 in recognition of the Franco-American friendship established during the American Revolution. On her completion, Liberty had to make her own journey over the Atlantic: she was dismantled and shipped to the US in 350 individual pieces in 214 crates, and was then rebuilt in 1886.

When the US opened up its borders to immigration in the 19th and early 20th centuries, it was this statue that the arriving hopefuls first saw before landing on Ellis Island where they were either allowed in or turned away.

JOURNEY'S END

Pamela Digby Churchill Hayward Harriman, Bill Clinton's Madame Ambassador to Paris, died doing laps in the pool at the Ritz where she used to meet her personal trainer every morning. This girl was quite a traveller: in the spirit of her great great great something aunt, Jane Digby, she'd started off travelling from Dorset to London, where she married Winston Churchill's son Randolph. She moved on to Paris (where she famously had an affair with Eli de Rothschild), to Italy (where she was 'great' friends with Gianni Agnelli) and then to America where she worked her way through men and states, ending up with Averill Harriman whom she'd first been involved with in London during World War II. After his death, her tireless devotion to the Democrat cause was rewarded with a ticket to the American Embassy in Paris, where she and her art collection were duly installed and remained until she died.

GREEN TRAVELLING

Travelling is more popular than ever, and with the proliferation of cheap and easy flights, people are visiting every far flung corner of the globe. Millions of people travelling worldwide has a huge impact on the environment. Air travel causes huge CO_2 emissions and airport expansion issues, to name just a few. On the other hand, tourism provides valuable income, jobs and foreign exchange to countries that would otherwise struggle economically. So the answer for the concerned traveller would seem to be to travel, but be aware of the impact it has.

Some organisations that can help green travellers plan a guilt-free holiday are:

> *www.responsibletravel.com*
> *www.tourismconcern.org.uk*
> *www.tearfund.org*

THE INTERNATIONAL DATELINE

Zigzagging across the waters of the Pacific Ocean near the 180-degree meridian, the International Date Line (IDL) is plotted on today's charts and globes to indicate the boundary line between 'today' and 'tomorrow'. But despite its name, the precise location of the IDL is not fixed by any international law, treaty or agreement.

Possibly the earliest reference to the date line is found in the works of Syrian prince and geographer-historian Abu'l-Fida (1273–1331). In his *Taqwin al-Buldan*, Abu'l-Fida described how a traveller, depending on his direction of travel, would either lose or gain a day at the completion of his circumnavigation.

It was Antonio Pigafetta (*c.*1490–*c.*1535), the chronicler of the first circumnavigation of the world by the Portuguese explorer and navigator Ferdinand Magellan (*c.*1480–1521), who first mentioned the peculiar incident of 'losing' a whole day.

A date line was adopted in the Pacific Ocean, but has only ever been defined by cartographers.

In October 1884, representatives from 25 countries met at the International Meridian Conference in Washington to recommend a common prime meridian for geographical and nautical charts that would be acceptable to all concerned.

Due to the lack of any international guidelines for the location of the date line, 20th-century mapmakers have tended to follow the recommendations of the British and the American Navy. The earliest recommendations issued by these departments referring to the date line appear to date from 1899 and 1900.

In 2000, Kiribati, an extended group of islands crossed by the IDL along its eastern boundary, became a serious contender in the race for the best place in the Pacific from which to view the first rays of the rising sun at the beginning of the new millennium.

The props department had done it again: Yorick was supposed to be a skull, not a scroll.

TRAVEL TEASERS

There was an airplane crash in which every single person died.
There were two survivors. How is this possible?
Answer on page 144

FANTASTIC FESTIVITIES

Festa de Sao Joao, Oporto, Portugal, *June*
This festival involves the townspeople running around and
hitting each other over the head with plastic hammers and
heads of garlic. The exact reasons for this are lost in time,
but the festival is practised every 23 and 24 June nonetheless. The whole town also turns out on the streets for bon-
fires, eating and drinking and the party lasts all night.

La Noche de Rabanos, Oaxaca, Mexico, *December*
The humble radish becomes the building block of life in
December, as inhabitants create animals, vehicles and
landscapes from this multi-talented vegetable. Inspiration
is fuelled throughout the day by tequila, and it's customary
to chuck your plate over your shoulder after tucking in.

THE SIGNS AREN'T GOOD

In a Tokyo Hotel:
Is forbidden to steal hotel
towels please. If you are
not a person to do such
thing is please not to read
notis.

**Two signs in a Bucharest
hotel lobby:**
The lift is being fixed for
the next day. During that
time we regret that you will
be unbearable.
To move the cabin, push
button for wishing floor. If
the cabin should enter more
persons, each one should
press a number of wishing

floor. Driving is then going
alphabetically by national
order.

In a Paris hotel elevator:
Please leave your values at
the front desk.

In a hotel in Athens:
Visitors are expected to
complain at the office
between the hours of 9 and
11am daily.

In a Yugoslavian hotel:
The flattening of underwear
with pleasure is the job of
the chambermaid.

SUFFERING FROM WIND

• The Atlantic hurricane season officially blows from 1 June to 30 November. These dates encompass over 97% of tropical gales, which reach their peak in early to mid September.

• The North-east Pacific basin receives its hurricane activity from late May or early June to late October or early November. The storms peak in late August or early September.

• The North-west Pacific basin suffers from tropical cyclones all year round, although there is a distinct drop in February and the first half of March and an increase from July to November, peaking in late August or early September.

• The North Indian basin has a double peak of hurricane activity in May and November, although tropical cyclones are also witnessed from April to December.

• The South-west Indian and Australian and South-east Indian basins have very similar annual cycles with tropical cyclones beginning in late October or early November and ending in May.

• The South-west Pacific basin begins its tropical cyclone activity in late October or early November. It reaches a single peak in late February or early March, and then fades out in early May.

• Globally, September is the most active month for hurricanes with May escaping the most unscathed.

DISTINCTIVE DWELLINGS

Cave hotel, Tunisia

Hotel Sidi Driss, one of 'les Troglodytes' (traditional underground cave dwellings), was used as the location of Luke Skywalker's home in the original Star Wars film. A typical Berber dwelling, the hotel has a central courtyard dug deep in the earth, surrounded by tunnels that lead to cave bedrooms and a cave restaurant.

INTERESTING FOREIGN SECRETARIES

19–22 December 1783: The 1st Marquess of Buckingham was the shortest serving Foreign Secretary.

1807–1089: George Canning had policy differences with his cabinet colleague Castlereagh (the Secretary of State for War) which led to a duel in which Canning was wounded in the leg. This is the last time cabinet ministers are known for sure to have fought it out.

1834–1835: The first Duke of Wellington's idea of foreign policy was to: 'stand well with France and distrust Russia'.

1886: Lord Rosebery achieved his three most treasured ambitions by the age of 48: he'd become Prime Minister, won the Derby and married an heiress.

1905–1916: Viscount Grey was the longest serving Foreign Secretary. It was from his room that he observed the 'lamps going out all over Europe'.

1935–1938: Sir Anthony Eden broadened the basis of recruitment into the Foreign Office so that you no longer had to be independently wealthy to serve there.

1938–1940: Lord Halifax; he once mistook Hitler for a doorman.

TRAVEL TEASERS

Where in Africa?
C
GO
Answer on page 144

21ST CENTURY NOMADS

The Innu are the traditional followers of the migrating herds of Canadian caribou in eastern Canada's Labrador peninsula. First they hunted them with spears and arrows, then with muskets and now with rifles. And these days, instead of walking to the hunting site or even riding there on a hunting sledge, they take snowmobiles or even fly there by helicopter. In winter, the herds of caribou roam the frozen, windswept plateau of the Barren Grounds. Here, in campsites, the hunters leave their tents at daybreak and share their catches at a communal feast at night. The feast won't necessarily consist just of caribou, but fish, game birds and even fox or roasted porcupine can be added to the menu.

Unfortunately, this is a lifestyle slowly being eroded as expeditions, such as those to hunt the caribou, become ever harder as the ancestral hunting grounds are violated by mining operations and swept by low-flying jets on training exercises.

WHO GOES WHERE?

	Visitors by year	
Algeria	1 million	*60% French 14% Italians*
Australia	2.5 million	*24% Japanese 19% other Asian*
China	4 million	*27% Japanese 13% USA*
France	70 million	*23% German 14% UK*
India	1.7 million	*14% British 13% Bangladeshis*
Israel	2.2 million	*23% USA 11% French*
Italy	20 million	*30% German 10% French*
Jamaica	1 million	*67% USA 14% Canadian*
Japan	3.5 million	*24% Korean 20% Taiwanese*
Russia	3 million	*17% Chinese 16% Finnish*
UK	18.5 million	*15% USA 13% French*
USA	45.6 million	*43% Canadian 19% Mexican*

Sukhotai, Thailand
Sukhotai, originally a Khmer settlement, was rebuilt around 1290 and was the centre of a wealthy kingdom until 1438. Thailand's first capital still boasts beautiful temple ruins, shrines and images of the walking Buddhas.

Mistras, Greece
From the early 1300s, Mistras flourished as a centre for Byzantine Renaissance. The philosopher Plethon lived here in the 1500s. He 'discovered' Plato and was the protege of the last Byzantine Emperor. Well-preserved churches and views of Sparta, once the military capital of the world, contribute to make this ruined city unique.

Santiago de Compostela, Spain
St James's body was rediscovered here in the 9th century, after being lost for 750 years. Santiago de Compostela became a great pilgrim centre, inspired the world's first travel guide and attracted more than 500,000 visitors each year during the 11th and 12th centuries. The cathedral shrine continues to draw many people, especially via the old walking routes through France and Spain.

Amalfi, Italy
Amalfi was once a renowned maritime trading republic. Two centuries after its beginnings in the 9th century, the Mariner's Compass was invented here and some of the largest ships on the Mediterranean were built to transport crusaders to the Holy Land. The town's architecture reflects its Arabic and Byzantine influences and a tradition in papermaking.

Machu Picchu, Peru
The city of the Incas was built in the 15th century at the height of the Inca Empire. Only rediscovered and exposed to the West in 1911, it escaped Spanish conquest and remains an awe-inspiring ruined city, perched 2,500m above sea level in the Andes.

During the Victorian era, the increasing prosperity of the British upper middle class led to a growth in travel and a corresponding demand for reliable travel information. In 1836, John Murray III of London wrote and published the first modern guidebook, initiating a wide-ranging and comprehensive series that dispensed accurate information and advice for the sophisticated and affluent traveller's journeys 'in season' and winter sojourns in warmer climates.

Carefully researched and written by well-educated Britons (or local experts writing in English) who were often prominent or destined to become so, *Murray's Handbooks* were the most popular guidebooks for British travellers in the 19th century.

In addition to practical information, advice, and itineraries set forth in abundant detail, the guides contained vivid accounts of abandoned ruins, tortuous journeys along primitive roads, and scenic marvels. The volumes also featured summaries of the nation's history, geography, demographics, culture, and climate, along with maps and plans.

Within individual countries there were sometimes separate series for different areas. For instance, there was a series for northern Germany and one for southern Germany. Similarly, there was a separate series on Paris and many series on the counties of Britain.

The soft, red covered handbooks have become much sought after collector's items. With their fine maps and interesting recommendations they are listed by antiquarian booksellers with a value of up to £750!

Competition for a burgeoning guidebook market was provided by the *Baedeker Guides*, first published in 1846, and later by the *Blue Guide* series with others quickly following suit.

CALL ME A CAB

The word 'cab' is short for Cabriolet – which means: small, two wheeled, horse-drawn carriage with two seats and a folding hood. A Hansom Cab was one which had the driver standing up behind the enclosed seat where the passenger sat.

The London black cab as we know it was introduced in 1958: with a 2.2 litre diesel engine, automatic gearbox and ability to turn a circle of 25ft (not quite a sixpence) it remained in constant production (with one or two modifications) till 1997 – making it one of the longest lived British motor designs.

To become a taxi driver and the owner of a coveted driver's badge you have to pass 'The Knowledge' – which can take up to four years!

Invented by John Hertz in 1915, the Yellow Cab Co is the oldest largest cab management company in the US. Hertz, a Chicago car dealer, hit upon the idea of starting a cab company when he found he had surplus returned cars when customers traded in their cars. He chose the colour yellow because he read a University of Chicago report that said yellow is the easiest colour to spot.

In Delhi, taxis with black and yellow livery have been the smart way to travel since the design of the Morris Oxford was exported and renamed the Ambassador in 1954. White versions of the car are still used by Government officials and VIPs.

The word 'Rickshaw' derives from the Japanese expression 'Ji riki' which means 'man powered vehicle'. It is said to have been invented in 1870 Japan by an American Missionary, Jonathan Gable, whose aim was to provide gainful employment for a poor man he knew. Within 20 years, the rickshaw was to be seen in such far-lung places as Durban, Calcutta and Simla and it's still to be seen (usually bicycle-powered) all over the world.

Tired
of the same old
vacation rounds?

Then come to
HAWAII~*this time!*

As the tide rolled in, the Olympic organisers began to reconsider the wisdom of introducing beach pole-vaulting to the games.

DISTINCTIVE DWELLINGS

Tented safari lodge, Zimbabwe
The roar of lions, trumpeting of elephants and chattering of monkeys can all be heard through the canvas walls of your tented rooms when staying at a wilderness lodge in Africa. The comfortable walk-in tents of Linkwasha Tented Camp, in Hwange Park, Zimbabwe, are set off the ground on teak platforms, and linked by raised walkways.

PIE IN THE SKY

One Lancashire couple never travel without one particular item: a 30year-old meat pie. 'Pie' has been with the couple on their journeys around the world, managing to take in the sights at Las Vegas five times, Barbados four times, and most of Europe, Kuwait and the Falkland Islands, amassing a total distance of 500,000 miles. It originated as a joke when the couple's neighbour, a baker, gave them a pie that had been left in the oven over night. Pie was introduced into the family and soon began accompanying them on their travels. The couple always send a postcard from Pie to Holland's Pies, the bakers where it was born.

TRAVELLING IN DISGUISE

John Simpson (1944–), the BBC's World Affairs Editor, has earned a reputation as one of the world's most experienced and authoritative journalists, in a BBC career spanning more than 30 years. He has reported from more than 100 countries across the globe, from 30 war zones, and has interviewed numerous world leaders. One of his most recent and demanding assignments was reporting from Afghanistan during the fall of Kabul. He was the first western journalist to go behind enemy lines in Taliban-controlled Afghanistan, before the war began.

He arrived on the back of a truck, disguised as a woman dressed in a blue burkha. Other close shaves include being attacked with poisonous gas in the Gulf, dodging the bullets in Tiananmen Square and being punched by former British Prime Minister Harold Wilson. When asked about his incessant travelling, he quotes Sir Richard Burton: 'Starting in a hollowed log of wood – some thousand miles up a river, with an infinitesimal prospect of returning, I ask myself, "Why?" and the only echo is, "Damned fool! The Devil drives".'

Killer earthquakes

Date	Place	Richter Scale	Number killed
27/07/1976	Tangshan, China *164,000 injured*	7.5	255,000– 655,000
01/09/1923	Kanto, Japan	7.9	143,000
05/10/1948	Ashgabat, Turkmenistan	7.3	110,000
28/12/1908	Messsina, Italy *Created a tsunami*	7.2	70,000– 100,000
31/05/1970	Peru	7.9	66,000
30/05/1935	Quetta, Pakistan	7.5	30,000– 60,000
26/12/2003	Bam, Iran	6.6	30,000
12/07/1988	Spitak, Armenia	6.8	25,000
19/09/1985	Michoacan, Mexico	8.0	9,500– 30,000
26/01/2001	Gujara, India *166,836 injured*	7.7	20,005
08/17/1999	Izmit, Turkey *50,000 injured, 500,000 homeless*	7.6	17,118
22/05/1960	Chile	9.5	4,000–5,000
26/12/2004	Indonesia *Created a tsunami*	9.1	283,000
8.10.2005	Pakistan	7.6	86,000

LEFT OR RIGHT?

When in 1923 Nova Scotia changed their driving habits from left to right, car owners put stickers on their windscreens to warn people who were heading for a head-on collision. However, it wasn't quite as easy to warn the oxen, who had been trained to walk on the left. So many oxen were killed in accidents that beef prices plummeted and 1923 became known as the 'year of free beef'.

BIBLE TOPS NEW CHART

What does God have to do with shower caps, sweets on the pillow and trouser presses? Apparently he's less useful than all of them. Travelling business executives consider the good book, distributed free by the Gideon Society, as the most useless item available in a hotel room, pipping pillows and presses to the post. It's not much of a surprise to find they preferred internet connections and phone chargers, but when it was revealed that only 2% said they wanted adult TV channels, the credibility of the whole survey was called into question. An almighty reprieve.

GREAT MIGRATIONS YOU DIDN'T KNOW ABOUT

• Lobsters in the Caribbean – walk in lines across the sea floor going to the deep during the hurricane season.

• Eels spend about 20 years in European rivers and ponds and are capable of crossing fields at night if it's wet, when they begin their great migration returning to the Sargasso Sea in the Caribbean where they were born and where they spawn and die. Their elvers, at about four inches long, set off on a marathon two to three year journey, swimming back to Europe at great depths in order to avoid surface currents.

• The Arctic Tern flies annually 14,000 miles from the White Sea to Western Australia.

TRAVEL TEASERS

What links Argentina, Australia, Botswana, Brazil, Chile, Madagascar, Mozambique, Namibia, Paraguay and South Africa?
Answer on page 144

AMONG THE WORST IN-FLIGHT
FILMS OF ALL TIME

Apollo 13 – 1995
Airplane – 1980
And I Alone Survived – 1978
Angel Flight Down – 1996
Back from Eternity – 1956
The Concorde Affair – 1980
Crash – 1978
Crash Landing – 1958
Crisis in Mid-air – 1979
Panic in the Skies – 1996
Skyjacked – 1972
Shootdown – 1988
Terror in the Sky – 1971

When Charlie's Angels *(2000) is shown as an in-flight movie, airlines remove the opening scene of the angels retrieving a bomb from a 747, opening the emergency door, and parachuting out.*

FANTASTIC FESTIVITIES

Day of the Dead, Mexico, *November*
El Dia De Los Muertos is the day of the dead in Mexico. This annual festival takes place on the 1st and 2nd of November (All Saints Day and All Souls Day), but rather than a simple day of mourning, it's a day of celebration with people preparing their favourite foods for absent friends. A traditional offering is the *pan de muerto*, which is a rich coffee cake decorated with meringues that resemble bones, skull-shaped sweets, marzipan death figures and skulls. The spirits are guided home by candles and flowers left on their graves and at 6pm the bells summoning the dead begin to ring, not stopping until sunrise.

CALL MY BLUFF,
MARITIME STYLE

Which of the following definitions is the correct one for
the following nautical names?

Davy Jones' Locker – the bottom of the ocean
1 A rather fierce pub owner named David Jones used to
incapacitate helpless drinkers in his ale locker and then
send them off on ships.
2 A derivation of the word devil.
3 Davy is a derivation of 'duffy', the West Indian term
for ghost, Jones comes from Jonah and a locker is a valuable place to store things, so the whole phrase means that
someone is safe with Duffy Jonah now.

**Jolly Roger – a pirate flag featuring skeletons, dagger,
cutlasses or bleeding hearts**
1 From the French term *joli rouge* meaning pretty red, to
describe the blood-stained flag flown above pirate ships.
2 An Indian pirate called Ali Raja who flew a red flag,
which English pirates called Alley Roger's flag. Alley could
have been subsequently changed to jolly.
3 Old Roger was a common name for the devil and also
an old English word for a vagabond or rogue.

**Blue Peter – a blue flag with a white square in the centre
indicating that the ship is ready to sail**
1 It is a corruption of blue repeater, one of the British
signal flags.
2 It is the international signal flag for the letter P.
3 Peter is a corruption of the French, *partir* (to leave).

Answer: Depends who you ask. Each of the above definitions is recognised as the true definition by at least one
authority.

10 ROAD TRIP CLASSICS

Six days on the Road	Dave Dudley
Mustang Sally	Wilson Pickett
I Can See for Miles	The Who
Crossroads	Cream
Roadhouse Blues	Doors
Truckin'	Grateful Dead
Country Roads (Take Me Home)	John Denver
Take it Easy	Eagles
Life in the Fast Lane	Eagles
Cars	Gary Numan

BEEN THERE, DONE THAT

Western explorers who were the first to...

Round the Cape of Good Hope:
Bartolomeu Diaz
Portuguese explorer 1488

Cross the Sahara:
Dixon Denham and Hugh Clapperton
English explorers 1822–23

Explore the Zambesi River:
David Livingstone
Scottish explorer 1851

Explore China:
Marco Polo
Italian traveller c.1272

Explore the Amazon River:
Francisco Orellana
Spanish explorer 1541

Explore Australia (first European to reach the area):
Abel Janszoon Tasman
Dutch navigator 1642

Cross Australia:
John McDouall Stuart
Scottish explorer 1862

Cross the Antarctic Circle:
James Cook
English navigator 1773

Reach the North Pole (controversial):
Robert E Peary
American explorer 1909

Reach the South Pole:
Roald Amundsen
Norwegian explorer 1911

An act of 1414, during the reign of Henry V, talks of the concept of 'Safe Conduct' with which one might travel abroad. Things became formalised when the Privy Council began granting passports in 1540. One of the earliest still in existence was issued on 18 June 1641, and was signed by Charles I. From 1644 to 1649, passes to British and foreign subjects were issued by the two Houses of Parliament. An order to the House of Commons dated 14 April 1649 directs that no pass should be granted to any person until he had first given an undertaking that he would not 'act, be aiding, assisting, advising or counselling against the Commonwealth'. Until the days of Charles II, the sovereign personally signed all British passports but in 1794, the Secretary of State took over the growing task. A record exists of all passports issued from that date.

By the outbreak of war in 1914 the price of a passport was 6d. The modern passport system dates from this time as states started issuing passports as a means of distinguishing their citizens from those considered to be foreign nationals. The first modern UK passport was issued in 1915 when the *British Nationality and Status of Aliens Act* 1914 came into force.

The old blue, 32-page British passport came into use as a result of a League of Nations International Conference on Passports after World War I. In the 1970s, increased overseas travel made security adaptation to passports necessary. Passports were issued for a single period of 10 years on 1 February 1968.

On 15 August 1988, the Passport Office began to produce the new style burgundy red, machine-readable UK passport. This became known as the MRP while the former hard-backed blue passport became known as 'Old Blues' – though the traditional features of the Royal Coat of Arms and the written requirement to allow the holder free passage and protection were retained.

The machine-readable strip on the details page enables immediate cross-referencing with immigration computers. The MRP also speeds up passage through frontier controls.

Some other security features of the new style passports are:

• A digitally-printed facial image of the holder, instead of a glued in photograph.

• A digital capture of the holder's signature.

• The personal identification page is protected by a clear laminate, which incorporates a transparent optically variable device that protects the portrait.

Today, approximately five million British passports are issued every year in the UK.

JUNGLE BOOK OF SURVIVAL

• Insects find the saltiness of sweat attractive. Cover up well, especially sweaty places like your armpits and groin. If ever you disturb a nest of bees or hornets, run!
• When camping, keep clothing and boots off the ground to stop snakes and insects nesting in them. Always shake well before putting them back on.
• If you find a hairy caterpillar climbing up your arm, brush it off in the direction it is climbing to stop its hairs sticking in your skin and causing a reaction.

• Mosquitoes are especially active at dawn and dusk. Cover your face, head and hands as well as the rest of your body to protect yourself from them. In camp, a smoky fire will help keep all insects away.
• Don't wash with soap: it removes natural oils in the skin which act as a natural barrier to water and germs. Save soap for when you need clean hands, such as when administering first aid – soap is a better antiseptic than iodine, which destroys skin as well as germs.

Egypt *and the* Mediterranean

Karaoke nights were quite the thing during the reign of Rameses II.

¿HABLAS ESPAÑOL?

• There are 21 Spanish-speaking countries in the world: Argentina, Bolivia, Chile, Colombia, Costa Rica, Cuba, Dominica Republic, Ecuador, El Salvador, Equatorial Guinea, Guatemala, Honduras, Mexico, Nicaragua, Panama, Paraguay, Peru, Puerto Rico, Spain, Uruguay and Venezuela.

• The total number of Spanish-speaking people in the world is 373.3 million. Mexico has the largest population with 93.7 million, the smallest is Equatorial Guinea with 0.5 million people.

• Brazil, whose 170 million inhabitants speak Portuguese, accounts for some 50% of the South American population.

Hadrian's Wall, Northern England

Despite the Romans victorious invasion of southern and central England, they were unable to conquer the northern tribes. In 122 AD, Emperor Hadrian had a massive defence fortification built from Newcastle to Carlisle to effectively 'divide and rule' the peoples of England. The remaining wall presents a significant testimony to the power of the Roman Empire.

Lake Lugu, Yunnan, China

Living on the nearly inaccessible idyllic Lake Lugu in the Eastern Himalayas, the Mosuo peoples represent the last matriarchy in Asia. Here, it is the women who own and inherit property, and run the businesses.

Oasis of Siwa, Egypt

Some 2,300 years ago, Alexander the Great came to Siwa, a luscious oasis, to consult the oracle at the Temple of Ammon. The Temple built atop a rocky hill, still dominates the town, surrounded by a mud-brick minaret and palm-shaded paths.

Palmyra, Syria

One of the richest cities of antiquity, Palmyra served as a trading post for Arab camel caravans on the Silk Trading Route linking the East and the West. The city was built on the Roman model, with an array of grand avenues, colonnades and fountains. It was home to Queen Zenobia, the woman who almost succeeded in supplanting Rome, but was captured in chains of gold, ending Palmyra's glory in 272 AD.

Taj Mahal, Agra, India

The Taj Mahal is a testimony to the Mughal's greatness during the 17th century. It took 20,000 men 20 years to build this beautiful marble mausoleum, in honour of Empress Mumtaz Mahal. Skilled craftsmen and precious stones for its interior were brought in from Europe through China to create a 'structure that evoked paradise itself'.

HOTEL HEISTS

Items hotels expect their guests will take:
Soaps • Shower caps • Shampoos • Stationery
Sewing kits • Tea bags • Coffee sachets

**Items that hotels really didn't want their guests to take,
but they have done nonetheless:**
Towels – the most commonly stolen item
Pillows • Bedspreads • Bed sheets • Blankets
Bathroom sinks • Reclining chairs • Safe deposit boxes
Ashtrays • Pictures and wall hangings
Televisions and video players
Irons and ironing boards
A six-and-a-half-foot high ficus tree

• The American Hotel and Lodging Association estimates that theft in hotel rooms costs the US leisure industry US$100 million every year.
• Holiday Inn loses 560,000 towels a year.
• One in five Americans have taken a hotel towel.
• A study of British hoteliers revealed that women are more likely to steal a towel than men: 66% of women admitted to a theft whereas only 59% of men admit their involvement in such a crime.

AKA

Nicknames of cities round the world

Paris, France	*City of Lights*
Rome, Italy	*City of the Seven Hills*
Manila, Philippines	*Pearl of the Orient*
Prague, Czech Republic	*City of a Hundred Spires*
Salzburg, Austria	*Festival City*
Berlin, Germany	*Millennium City*

SURVIVAL TIPS

Stranded on a desert island?
• Most seaweeds are edible but avoid any that are blue-green and growing in fresh or stagnant water as they are extremely poisonous.
• Avoid all filter feeders such as mussels as they concentrate toxins especially in the summer months.
• Avoid cone shells in the tropics as they can shoot poisonous barbs sufficiently toxic to kill a man.
• In a survival situation, cook all shellfish.
• Avoid going into the water barefoot as you might tread on poisonous spiny animals.
• When eating crab make sure it is cooked and that the lungs or 'dead men' are removed as these are poisonous.
• Try and fish from the windward side of an island; the fish in a lagoon are often poisonous varieties or their eating habits cause them to be toxic.
• Coconuts provide food and water but too much coconut is a powerful purgative, especially the very young green or old brown nuts. Eat and drink in moderation.

LEFT OR RIGHT?

Contrary to popular tradition, jousters always rode on the right carrying their lances with their strong right arms so that they could attack their opponents across their bodies on the left. The reason people used to drive on the left is that it's easier to control a horse with the right arm. If you were walking with a cart you wouldn't want to be in the middle of the road, you'd put the horse there. You also mount and dismount a horse from the left because you'd wear your sword on you left side so you can draw it easily with your right arm. And if you were attacked on the road it would be easier if you were on the left for the same sword-drawing reasons. Which is why we drive on the left.

MARY, MARY, QUITE CONTRARY

In 1892, aged 30, Mary Kingsley set off for West Africa where she planned to research African religions and laws in order to finish a book her uncle, Charles Kingsley, had left unfinished at his death. Between 1893 and 1894 she travelled to Angola, Nigeria and the islands of Fernando Po, collecting booty which was gratefully accepted by the Natural History section of the British Museum. She also travelled in the Congo and previously unexplored parts of Gabon.

She wrote prolifically, always expressing her deep affection for African people. Of the Fan people whom she encountered in 1894 during her ascent of the Ogowe river in Gabon, she wrote in *Travels in West Africa:* 'I must not forget to mention the other member of our party, a Fan gentleman with the manners of a duke and the habits of a dustbin. He came with us, quite uninvited by me, and never asked for any pay: I think he only wanted to see the fun, and drop in for a fight if there was one going on, and to pick up the pieces generally. He was evidently a man of some importance, from the way the others treated him; and moreover he had a splendid gun, with a gorilla skin sheath for its lock, and ornamented all over its stock with brass nails. His costume consisted of a small piece of dirty rag round his loins; and whenever we were going through dense undergrowth, or wading a swamp, he wore that filament tucked up scandalously short. Whenever we were sitting down in the forest having one of our nondescript meals, he always sat next to me and appropriated the tin. Then he would fill his pipe, and turning to me with the easy grace of aristocracy, would say what may be translated as "My dear Princess, could you favour me with a Lucifer?" I used to say, "My dear Duke, charmed, I'm sure," and give him one ready lit.'

DEAD SEA? DYING SEA

The Dead Sea is landlocked between Jordan and Israel at the lowest point of the earth, some 400m below sea level. Bathers can enjoy the strange sensation of floating unaided in the extremely salty water. But maybe not for much longer. The popular tourist attraction is in fact shrinking. It is estimated that the water level has dropped by more than 130ft in the last 50 years and it is still dropping by as much as three feet per year in recent times. The area of the sea is now a third less than it was a century ago. It is thought that the water is disappearing as a result of commercial siphoning.

You couldn't storm up and down the Dead Sea exhibiting a punishing crawl: the water's so salty you'd burn your eyes. There are signs all around the bathing places warning people to keep the water out of their eyes. The other phenomenon which isn't often mentioned is its stink produced by its sulphurous mud (which is supposed to have all sorts of beneficial qualities).

TRAVEL TIPS

It can be difficult to enter some countries, if another country has stamped your passport. The US, for example, is notoriously difficult for visitors arriving from Cuba. Find out before you enter a country if their stamp might impede your travels later and if so, ask NICELY if they wouldn't mind stamping a piece of paper instead.

TRAVEL TEASERS

A French plane carrying Spanish passengers from Germany to Canada crashes in the sea between Ireland and America. Where do they bury the survivors?
Answer on page 144

THE ANCIENT WONDERS OF THE WORLD

The list of the Seven Wonders of the Ancient World was originally compiled around the 2nd century BC although the first reference is found in Herodotus' *Histories* in the 5th century BC. The list we know today was compiled in the Middle Ages despite hardly any of the Wonders actually surviving as long as this.

Pyramids of Giza

A gigantic stone structure near the ancient city of Memphis. It is the only Wonder still standing, despite being the oldest, having been built around 2560 BC.

Hanging Gardens of Babylon

The gardens in question were connected with a palace built on the banks of the River Euphrates, near Baghdad by King Nebuchadnezzar II.

Statue of Zeus at Olympia

A huge statue of the Greek god of gods, sculpted by Pheidias at the ancient town of Olympia, on the west coast of modern Greece. The statue was destroyed after the Olympic games were deemed Pagan practices in 391 AD and banned by Emperor Theodosius I.

Temple of Artemis at Ephesus

A beautiful temple in the ancient city of Ephesus near the modern town of Selcuk, in Turkey. It was erected in honour of the Greek goddess of hunting around 550 BC. On the night of 21 July 356 BC, Herostratus burned the temple to the ground.

Mausoleum of Maussollos at Bodrum, modern Turkey

A fascinating tomb constructed in 350 BC for King Maussollos, Persian satrap (provincial governor) of Caria in the city of Bodrum on the Aegean Sea, in south-west Turkey. The tomb survived for 16 centuries until an earthquake destroyed the roof and colonnade.

Colossus of Rhodes

This huge statue of Helios

the sun god was erected at the entrance to the harbour in Rhodes. The construction of the Colossus took some 12 years to complete and was finally finished in 282 BC. For years, the giant statue stood guard at the harbour entrance, until a strong earthquake hit Rhodes in about 226 BC. The city was badly damaged, and the Colossus was broken at its weakest point (the knees) and it fell.

The Lighthouse at Alexandria

Built by the Ptolemies on the island of Pharos, off the coast of their capital city, this lighthouse ensured a safe return for sailors navigating the difficult waters. It was the world's tallest building at the time and was conceived around 290 BC by Ptolemy Soter. Destroyed by earthquakes over the centuries, it used fire at night and reflected sunlight during the day.

A RUM FELLOW

Captain Morgan, a familiar face to rum drinkers, has adorned thousands of bottles of original spiced rum. Unlike many brand characters, however, Captain Morgan did actually exist.

Sir Henry Morgan (1635–1688) was essentially a pirate, but a pirate with some very influential friends. Based in Jamaica, he was able to take advantage of the fact that Britain had a valuable province but no way of defending it. The Crown back in London were at the time relying on privateers and buccaneers to protect the island. Although King Charles II claimed to not know about this state-funded piracy, Morgan was able to grow wealthy from just such a role. He carried on with plundering and looting until he was arrested and taken back to London. However he was soon knighted and reinstated to his duties in Jamaica where he continued to patrol the Caribbean until his death in 1688.

ENGLAND
the daily pageant

Lionel knew he could conquer the world, now that he had successfully cloned an army of vicious beefeaters.

TRAVEL TEASERS

Where in America?
NESOMTA
Answer on page 144

FANTASTIC FESTIVITIES

Kattenwoensdog, Ypres, Belgium, *May*

Over 200 years ago, this Belgian town was overrun with mice. To solve the problem, the resourceful locals brought in cats. However, once the mice were dealt with, the locals had a self-induced cat plague to deal with. Rather than finding an animal willing to hunt down the felines the residents decided to take matters into their own hands, literally. They caught the cats and threw them off the top of a tall tower. Today the festival still involves tabby tossing, but of the fluffy and fake variety. So, if you have an aversion to cats then perhaps you should head to the belfry of the Cloth Hall on the second Sunday in May. Every other year, the cat hurling is complemented with parades celebrating famous cats.

FASTEST RAIL JOURNEYS

	Journey, *Country*	Distance (km)	(miles)	Speed (km/h)	(mph)
1	Hiroshima–Kokura, *Japan*	192	119.3	261.8	162.7
2	Valence–Avignon, *France*	129.7	80.6	259.4	161.2
3	Brussels Midi–Valence, *Belgium and France*	831.3	516.5	242.1	150.4
4	Madrid–Seville, *Spain*	470.5	292.4	209.1	129.9
5	Stendal–Wolfsburg, *Germany*	76.2	47.3	190.4	118.3
6	York–Stevenage, *UK*	258	160.3	182.8	113.6
7	Skovde–Sodertalje, *Sweden*	277	172.1	173.1	107.6
8	Rome–Florence, *Italy*	261	162.2	166.6	103.5
9	Baltimore–Wilmington, *USA*	110.1	68.4	165.1	102.6
10	Salo–Karjaa, *Finland*	53.1	33	151.7	94.3

MIND HOW YOU GO

The most dangerous road in the world, according to the Association for Safe International Travel, is in Bolivia. This popular tourist trail starts at 4,700m in the mountains and descends 3,600m over 60 miles to the rainforest and jungle below. A vehicle, usually a truck or passenger bus, goes off the side of the road about once a fortnight.

The road, which links La Paz and the Yungas, is mostly made up of a one-lane dirt track with regular intervals cut into the cliff. If two vehicles meet then one has to reverse until there is room to get past. The Andean drivers of the buses follow a variety of rituals to keep them safe on the death-defying trail, including splashing their tyres with alcohol to bless the vehicle. To increase their chances of making the journey alive they also make offerings of coca leaves and build little rock cairns.

HERO FOR HIRE

Travelling solo is not everyone's idea of a dream getaway. Some people prefer a good chinwag and a buddy to share the journey with. But what if your friends prefer popping to the corner shop rather than a 20-hour train ride across India or a hike through the Andes? Well, a new escort service for women has solved this problem by offering men for hire to share holidays and travels. For £3,000 the woman gets attention and pampering on demand for her trip. The agency was the brain child of ex-model Steve Jarsman from Perth who capitalised on women's desire for their boyfriends to be willing to join them round the world and fawn over them on the way. Escorts in Paradise hopes to bring women's desires for romantic travel and fantasy alive. Jarsman adds that: 'client's pay for an escorts's time. If a lady wants to take the relationship further, and 80% of them do, then that's between her and the escort.'

OLD ROAD TO CHINA

If you were hitching a camel ride from Syria to China, around 1425, this is the route you would take:

Aleppo, Damascus, Babylon, Selencia, Ecbatane, Merv, Bukhara, Samarkand, Kashgar, Yarkand, Cherchen, Dunhuang, Changian

HISTORIC HOLIDAYS

The Lascaux Cave, Dordogne, France
Discovered by accident in 1940, this 15,000-year-old cave contains striking paintings of horses and wild oxen as well as the tools that the artists used. The original is now closed, but this testimony of the Stone Age can still be experienced in a replica nearby.

Ryoangi Rock Garden, Kyoto, Japan
15th century Japanese culture is delicately portrayed in this kare-sansui (dry landscape) garden. Fifteen rocks are grouped in small islands on a sea of white gravel. The garden is a reflection of Zen Buddhism, indeed, only with enlightenment can one see the 15th-century rock.

Visby, Gotland, Sweden
Once a Stone Age sacrificial site, Visby was resettled by the Vikings in the 6th century. They used it as a base for trading routes to Asia and developed it into a medieval stronghold. The 1350s saw a plague that killed more than 8,000 people, and although it was refurbished by the Germans, the Pearl of the Baltic or the City of Roses never regained its status.

Borobudur, Jogjakarta, Indonesia
The giant stupa Borobudur, built during the 8th and 9th centuries lies in the Indonesian jungle. The shrine is arranged in nine 2.5km-long terraces, embellished by hundreds of Buddha statues and friezes.

A lot of people have been on an aeroplane. And a lot of people have heard the safety announcements one too many times. Sometimes the airline staff attempt to liven up these and other announcements by adding their own little touch. Here are some examples that have been heard or reported:

On a flight with a very 'senior' flight attendant crew: 'Ladies and gentlemen, we've reached cruising altitude and will be turning down the cabin lights. This is for your comfort and to enhance the appearance of your flight attendants.'

'To operate your seat belt, insert the metal tab into the buckle, and pull tight. It works just like every other seat belt; and, if you don't know how to operate one, you probably shouldn't be out in public unsupervised.'

And from the pilot during his welcome message: 'This airline is pleased to have some of the best flight attendants in the industry. Unfortunately, none of them are on this flight!'

'In the event of a sudden loss of cabin pressure, masks will descend from the ceiling. Stop screaming, grab the mask, and pull it over your face. If you have a small child travelling with you, secure your mask before assisting with theirs. If you are travelling with more than one small child, pick your favourite.'

'As you exit the plane, make sure to gather all of your belongings. Anything left behind will be distributed evenly among the flight attendants. Please do not leave children or spouses.'

'Your seat cushions can be used for flotation; and in the event of an emergency water landing, please paddle to shore and take them with our compliments.'

On landing: 'Please be sure to take all your belongings with you when you leave the plane. If you're going to leave anything, please ensure it's something we'd like to have.'

THE 10 MOST POPULAR ADVENTURE TRAVELLING ACTIVITIES

1. Walking, hiking and trekking
2. Cycling
3. Cross-country skiing
4. Dog sledging
5. Horse riding
6. White-water rafting
7. Kayaking and sea-kayaking
8. Mountaineering and climbing
9. Scuba diving
10. Off-road driving

MURPHY'S LAWS FOR FREQUENT FLYERS

• No flight ever leaves on time unless you are running late and need the delay to make the flight.

• If you are running late for a flight, it will depart from the farthest gate within the terminal.

• If you arrive very early for a flight, it inevitably will be delayed.

• Flights never leave from Gate One at any terminal in the world.

• If you must work on your flight, you will experience turbulence as soon as you touch pen to paper.

• If you are assigned a middle seat, you can determine who has the seats on the aisle and the window while you are still in the boarding area. Just look for the two largest passengers.

• Only passengers seated in window seats ever have to get up to go to the lavatory.

• The crying baby on board the flight is always seated next to you.

• The strength of the turbulence is directly proportional to the temperature of your coffee.

• The less carry-on luggage space available on an aircraft, the more carry-on luggage passengers will bring aboard.

TRAVELLING IN DISGUISE

Sir Richard Francis Burton (1821–1890) was an explorer, linguist, diplomat, anthropologist, and a gifted writer. He wrote essays and books about everything he saw, and every place he visited, from Asia through Africa to South America. He discovered the source of the Nile, translated the *Kama Sutra* and the *Arabian Nights*, and was knighted by Queen Victoria. However, he is best known as a master of disguise. Starting as an undercover intelligence officer during the Sikh War, he perfected his ability in language and disguise. His most famous feat was infiltrating Mecca and the Medina in 1853. Disguised as an Afghan physician, he was the first 'infidel' to kiss the Kaaba. He had to perform almost hourly ceremonials, in which, had he failed to pay attention to detail, he would have been torn to pieces. Unsatisfied with this victory, Burton set out to enter the forbidden Muslim city of Harar, in Somalia. All non-believers who had entered this city before him had been executed, and Burton became the first white man to enter and leave alive.

DISTINCTIVE DWELLINGS

Floating luxury, Paris, France

Step on board *La Vie en Rose*, a luxury *peniche*, or river-boat, in the heart of Paris. Moored on the River Seine between the Ile St Louis and the Left Bank, La Vie en Rose is just upstream from Notre Dame cathedral. The floating hotel has a glass-walled sitting room and fully-fitted bathroom, but only one bedroom, making it the perfect hideaway for two. A full breakfast is provided every morning, and teatime snacks await hungry travellers after a day spent sightseeing or shopping. And here's the sign of true extravagance – maid service not once, but twice a day. Truly a rosy existence, as the name implies.

PASSPORT, TICKETS, CAMERA, KETCHUP

Going away can be about the joy of different places and the experiencing of alien cultures and meeting new people. However, everyone can be prone to a little homesickness. But what if a call home or a photo of a loved one is not enough? Well, you can always take the next step and take a piece of home with you.

Travellers have admitted that they like to take a piece of Britain with them when they are in foreign climes. And what they take can say something about what people really like about 'home'.

More than anything people want to be reminded of British food. Often derided as the worst cuisine of the world, Brits can't get enough of it while travelling the globe. And while its hard to take fish and chips, a Sunday roast or even a chicken tikka masala, people are making do with what comes in handy rucksack sized containers. According to a recent survey, the item most people take with them is tomato ketchup. Teabags from home are a more expected addition to the packing, and what is nicer than a few biscuits with your cuppa? Cornflakes, marmite and baked beans also made the list of home comforts.

I'VE BEEN HERE BEFORE...

Many people dream of spending time in some far-away foreign place, but few imagine they have already lived in a country they've never set foot in. Jesper Bood, a 29-year-old Swedish man who had never been to Scotland, was hypnotised for a documentary about reincarnation and claimed to have lived in the East Lothian town of Dunbar in the 1860s. He was able to describe the town in amazing detail and drew a map of the town blindfolded.

OLD POSTER, NEW CAPTION

*Three years after being allowed to paint her, Whistler was
beginning to regret the deal he'd made with his mother.*

TIME TRAVELLER CHECKS

We all know what we'd do if we had a time travel
machine (besides fainting, shouting, jumping up and
down etc), as Marty realised in *Back To The Future*: come
back from the future with all the information you need to
make a million.

When Andrew Carlssin turned a stock market investment
of US$350 into a portfolio valued at more than US$800
million in two weeks, he was arrested by federal investiga-
tors. He explained, in his defence, that he had come back
from the year 2256 when everyone knew that our era suffered one of the worst stock plunges in history. Apparently
the Security and Exchange Commission didn't believe him.
So now all he needs is the Doc to come and rescue him.

FRENCH FRIED

In 1950, French senator and former witch-doctor Victor Biaka-Boda travelled to the Ivory Coast, which he represented, to assess the electorate's concerns and drum up their support. They obviously liked the look of him because they ate him, but it's not clear whether he went down well.

SIGNS OF A SEASONED TRAVELLER

• All your passport pages have been used up. It's quicker to list the countries you haven't been to.
• You have friends in countries that your friends from home haven't even heard of.
• The travel supplement in the Sunday paper is more a trip down memory lane than an inspiration for your next holiday.
• The staff at Heathrow know you by name.
• You have been medically classified as resistant to all known diseases on account of all the immunisation injections you've received.
• You have enough frequent flier miles to get to the moon.
• Your lifetime guaranteed rucksack is giving up the will to live.
• You've written the equivalent of a small novel on the back of postcards.
• You feel more comfortable when sleeping on a bunk bed in a room with 12 other people from eight different countries.

COMIC TIMING

Can elephants run? The majestic beasts are accused of 'running' like Groucho Marx by John Hutchinson of Stanford University, California. However, even at top speed all four feet never leave the ground at once, which is, technically, walking.

NOT THE SHARPEST TRAVELLER
IN THE BOX

Ever had one of those days where you have become convinced that the general public perhaps lack a little common sense? Workers at tourist information centres around the UK seem to have become entirely convinced that the general public have actually never been even remotely acquainted with common sense, general knowledge or indeed the ability to manage with daily life. The English Tourism Council and Visit Scotland have released a list of 'quirky' enquiries they have received over the years. Included on the list are such diverse questions as:

• Is Dorking something English people do?
• What time does the Lake District open?
• What time do the UFOs fly, where can we sit and watch them and would it be all right to bring a picnic?
• I understand there is a gorilla breeding establishment somewhere in the South of England. Please could you tell me where it is because I want to take my wife there as a surprise?
• What time does the 10.20am bus run?
• Can I change my English currency into Scottish currency?
• Exactly where on the map does the Scottish accent stop and the English one start?
• Can you give me a list of garages selling petrol between Stoke-on-Trent and Windsor?
• What day is the New Years Day Parade on?
• How does the snow get up on Ben Nevis?
• How do you get to Brigadoon?
• Where are the Northern Lights and what time do they get turned on?
• Is Fort William still alive?

Oh dear.

FREE WHEELING

So if you want to travel the world for a while, a long while, how on earth do you pay for it? You could always go for Ramon Stoppelenburg's way. The Dutch student simply asked people if they would be willing to put him up for the night as he passed through. His website www.letmestayforaday.com led to an unexpectedly long trip around the world. Ramon received 3,577 invitations from 72 countries since setting off from his home in Zwoller in early 2001. In return for his accommodation he posted accounts of his travels on his website.

Ramon says that he had no idea what to expect when he established the site, although he thought that he would not get much further than his home town. The response was huge however and so off he went. He managed to travel for a year and a half without spending any money at all. Strangers helped him with accommodation and food and even with transport, sponsoring his travel and using their frequent flier miles to help him out. When that failed he hitchhiked. Just goes to show you what you can do with a little help from your friends. Or at least people you've never met but who have visited your website.

BON VOYAGE

If you don't want to say it in French...

Spanish	*El viaje bueno*
German	*Gute Reise*
Italian	*Buon viaggio*
Dutch	*Sloeg reis op*
Norwegian	*Bon sjøreise*
Portuguese	*A viagem de bo*
Danish	*Heldig rejse*
Finnish	*Iloinen matkustaa*
Welsh	*'N ddedwydd fordwya*
Latin	*Gauisus navigatio*

• If you want to send smoke signals first find a clearing in which to make your fire. Smoke will otherwise be hidden by the tree canopy. You could equally make a fire to send smoke signals from a raft on a river.

• In the jungle, it's very important to keep your feet covered to protect them from flesh-eating chigoes and centipedes, and leeches. Use bark or cloth to wrap legs from boots upwards to protect them.

• Leeches do not have a painful bite so when one attaches itself to you, you might not notice. To get rid of a leech use a dab of salt, the end of a cigarette or a match flame and it'll drop off: never pull a leech off the skin as you might leave the head behind, buried under your skin, and that will probably go septic.

• To make your fire you'll need to find dry tinder. The inside of standing dead wood will work well. So will dry bamboo and termites' nests.

• The infamous candiru is a tiny catfish which will, extremely rarely, swim up the urethra of someone peeing in a river. So, at the risk of stating the obvious… don't pee when you're standing deep in jungle water.

FANTASTIC FESTIVITIES

Skirt-lifting Festival, San Pablo de los Montes,
Spain, *January*

It's the one date all the men in the town never forget, but still the women are not impressed, for this is the fiesta of St Paul – the day when men can go around lifting up girls' skirts without getting battered over the head for indecent behaviour. However, one unfortunate man is picked each year to be dressed as 'la Madre Cochina' (the Old Bat), tarted up, paraded and molested by all and sundry.

SOME USEFUL INTERNATIONAL HELLOS

Arabic ....*Marhaba*
Cherokee ....*O'siyo*
Farsi ....*Salaam*
French ....*Bonjour*
German ....*Guten Tag*
Greek ....*Geia Sou*
Hawaiian ....*Aloha*
Hebrew ....*Shalom*
Hungarian ....*Sziasztok*
Irish ....*Dia duit*

TRAVELLING IN DISGUISE

Peter the Great (1672–1725) is best known for engineering a series of reforms that put Russia among the major European powers. He was inspired by a two-year Grand Tour of Europe, which he undertook in 1697. Under the name of Peter Mikhailov, he accompanied an embassy to European courts, disguised as a ship's carpenter, seaman, soldier, barber and, to the discomfort of his courtiers, as a dentist. The official purpose of the tour was to meet monarchs and conduct diplomacy, but he amassed a large body of knowledge on western European industrial techniques and state administration. He became determined to modernise the Russian state and to westernise its society and invited the best European engineers, architects, craftsmen and merchants to come to Russia and sent hundreds of Russians to Europe to receive the best education. In 1703, he built the new capital of St Petersburg on the recently conquered Gulf of Finland, enabling access to European sea trade. The 'tsar-reformer' also banned traditional Muscovite dress for all men, introduced military conscription and built the Russian Navy, established technical schools, simplified the alphabet and changed the calendar.

THE BIG TWO

The first Lonely Planet guide was called *Across Asia on the Cheap,* the brainchild of Maureen and Tony Wheeler who put it together at their kitchen table. At the time it was groundbreaking as it was custom made for the newly emerging backpackers who wanted to travel all over the world. It was published in 1973 and sold 8,000 copies in just three months in Australia and New Zealand. Spurred on by their success, they set about writing the follow up, *South-East Asia on a Shoestring* in a back street hotel in Singapore. The series has developed a lot since then, selling more than 5.5 million books a year in 118 countries.

The name Lonely Planet actually came about from a misunderstanding. Tony thought that Joe Cocker was singing 'lonely planet' when he was really singing 'lovely planet' in 'Space Captain'. Which might have been a slightly nicer spin.

Rough Guides were started by disgruntled student Mark Ellingham who decided that his guidebook to Greece was a bit rubbish and that he could probably do a lot better. So, he got a typewriter and put together a guide with a group of friends. It came out in 1981 and offered an insight into politics, geography and contemporary life with an honest and practical approach to traveller's needs and the local area. The series now covers 200 destinations around the globe.

FIVE FEARS TO GET YOU TRAVELLING

Claustrophobia ....enclosed spaces
Omatophobia, oikophobia ....home
Ecophobia ....home surroundings
Thaasophobia ....sitting idle
Eremophobia ....stillness

WHAT YOU DIDN'T PRESUME
ABOUT LIVINGSTONE

He was born in 1813 into a poor Scottish family and
worked in a cotton factory from the age of 10.

He never went to school.

Self taught, he studied geology and botany as well as
medicine until he had enough knowledge to qualify for his
medical diploma.

In 1840, he was sent by the Missionary Society of London
to Botswana not only to practise Evangelism but also to
preach against the slave trade which still existed with
Arab traders from the North.

At first he didn't travel alone. In 1849, the party for
his first exploration included his wife, three children and
several friends.

His various journeys made him the first European to cross
southern Africa from west to east.

FANTASTIC FESTIVITIES

Camel Wrestling Championship, Selcuk, Turkey, *January*
The Turkish answer to bullfights and cockfights, this
involves getting two bull camels in an arena and parading
a female to get them feeling macho. It's easy to tell when
a bull is getting excited, as milky saliva streams from
their mouth and nostrils. The bulls normally butt each
other half-heartedly until one runs away – and the crowd
then try to avoid a tonne of camel headed their way.

Cheese Rolling, Gloucester, *end of May*
A seven pound lump of cheese is rolled down a 300 yard-
high slope at Cooper's Hill, with a gradient of 2 in 1.
Contestants roll down after it. Winner takes the cheese.

OLD POSTER, NEW CAPTION

Waking from her deep sleep, the Statue of liberty realised she had floated straight up a Norwegian fjord.

PACK IT IN

When travelling, it's not always possible to lug around your worldly goods, so a day-pack is a must. Here is a list of essential items for a 21st-century day-pack:

- passport
- water bottle
- small, light, folding waterproof
- a power bar for emergency rations
- a local language book for entertaining guides
- small amount of cash
- spare photographic film
- a large handkerchief
- sarong or pashmina for cover up situations
- a plastic bag (multipurpose: to sit on, fill with rubbish, put wet things in)
- plasters
- dark glasses
- camera
- note book for astonishing journal entries
- a clip of safety pins (multipurpose: from laundry to gifts)
- small folding knife
- sun hat

Any more than this and it can't be termed a day-pack!

THE WOMAN BEHIND THE MAN

When arctic and antarctic explorer Ranulph Fiennes' wife first suggested he go round the world from top to bottom instead of side to side he replied: 'no sane person even tries to do it. If it were possible it would have been done. All oceans have been crossed west to east, north to south, solo, on rafts, backwards and sideways. All major mountains have been climbed and all rivers travelled up to their source and back down again. People have gone round the world by horse, bicycle and probably by broomstick. They have parachuted from over 30,000ft and gone paddling to the deepest spots in the deepest seas. Quite apart from strolling around on the moon.'

She was unimpressed. 'You're saying it can't be done because it hasn't been done. Is that it? That's pathetic.'

-OLOGISTS WHO MAY WANT TO TRAVEL

Anthropologist – Study and analysis of the origins and characteristics of human beings and their societies, customs and beliefs.

Archaeologist – Excavation and subsequent study of the physical remains of earlier civilisations, especially buildings and artefacts, which now benefits from advances in scientific techniques such as carbon dating.

Deltiologist – Study and collection of picture postcards.

Dialectologist – Study of dialect.

Egyptologist – Study of the language, culture and history of ancient Egypt.

Ethnologist – Scientific study of different races and cultural traditions, and their relationships.

Sinologist – Study of China in all its aspects, especially cultural and political.

AVOIDING JET LAG

Jet lag affects 94% of long-haul flyers and includes such physical symptoms as fatigue, insomnia, disorientation, swelling limbs, ear/nose/eye irritations, headaches, bowel irregularity and lightheadedness. Jet lag occurs because changes in time zones confuse the body's 24-hour inner clock known as 'circadian rhythms'.

• Avoid caffeine or alcohol.

• Isocones (pushing acupressure points) help you sleep during the journey.

• Travel west is best: arrive in the late afternoon if possible because then you don't have to wait long till bedtime and will be fresh the following morning.

• If travelling east arrive in the morning – and try to get straight into the sunlight as the body clock takes its timing from natural sunlight and will adjust eastwards more quickly.

• Adapt to your new time zone as quickly as possible, especially at meal and sleep times.

• Adjust your sleep time before you leave on your trip. If you are flying from the west coast to the east coast of America, for example; if your normal bedtime is midnight, then three nights before you travel go to sleep at 11pm. Two days before you travel, retire at 10pm, and the night before your trip, go to sleep at 9pm, (which is midnight on the east coast).

• Change your watch to your destination time zone on the plane. Sleep on the plane if it is bedtime in your arrival city; stay awake if it isn't.

• One authority, which thinks that dehydration is the main culprit of jet lag, recommends that you drink two glasses of water before getting on the plane and one or more litres in flight.

• One German study found sedentary passengers suffered more jet lag than those who walked or exercised. Exercise, both in the air and upon arrival, will circulate your blood and help you feel rejuvenated.

JOY RIDES

To become a member of the notorious Mile High Club, you need to engage in sexual intercourse while in an aeroplane, at least a mile above the earth's surface. Most people, although unsure of their exact altitude will claim to be members of this club having taken part in some kind of hanky-panky in a plane's lavatory.

This high altitude high-risk hobby can perhaps be traced back to a daring pilot in 1916. Lawrence Sperry grew up handsome and rich and his wild lifestyle earned him a regular place in the tabloids of the time. In November 1916 he began to give flying lessons to a New York socialite called Mrs Waldo Polk, whose husband was conveniently away driving an ambulance in France at the time. The pair became involved in some airborne antics, thanks to the newly devised autopilot. Unfortunately something went wrong with the plane and it plunged 500ft into the bay below. Rescuers were amazed to find that the couple had survived, albeit without clothing. Sperry claimed that the crash had divested them of their clothing but later confessed to causing the crash by knocking the gyro during a romantic encounter.

The tabloids, true to form, recognised a catchy headline a mile off and the *New York Mirror* and *Evening Graphic* ran with 'Aerial Petting Ends in Wetting'. They don't write 'em like they used to.

TRAVEL TEASERS

A train leaves from New York City heading toward Los Angeles at 100mph. Three hours later, a train leaves from Los Angeles heading toward New York City at 200mph. Assuming there are exactly 2,000 miles between Los Angeles and New York City. As they pass each other, which train is closer to New York City?
Answer on page 144

TEN MOST POPULAR SOUVENIRS, NOT SO POPULAR WITH CITES' ENDANGERED SPECIES CONVENTION

1. Crocodile skin products from Thailand and the USA
2. Rock python skin products from Africa
3. Coral from South-east Asia and the Caribbean
4. Conch shells and clams from the Caribbean
5. Ivory and elephant products from Africa and Asia
6. Hippo teeth from Africa and Asia
7. Turtle shell products from Sri Lanka, UAE and the Caribbean
8. Furs and skins from the big cats of South America and Africa
9. Parrots and toucans from China, Hong Kong and Thailand
10. Water monitor lizard's skin products from Asia and Nigeria

CITES (Convention on International Trade on Endangered Species) The 'Washington' Convention on International Trade in Endangered Species of Wild Fauna and Flora was launched in 1975 to protect endangered plants and animals. By controlling and overseeing their international trade, CITES seeks to prevent it reaching irreversible levels. More than 150 parties ratified the Convention, regulating international trade in over 30,000 species. CITES is administered by the United Nations Environment Programme (UNEP).

BUSK OR BUST

A 29-year-old full time busker from North Wales decided in 2004 to take his music to a wider audience by busking around the world. Nigel Ashcroft travelled only using the earnings from his busking, taking in Moscow, Barcelona, Hong Kong, Tokyo, Berlin, New York and Bangkok and delivering his repertoire of guitar-based performances.

TRAVELLERS' CHECKLIST

To make sure you are well prepared and have a safe holiday, the 10 most important things to do according to the Foreign and Commonwealth Office are:

• Check the Foreign and Commonwealth Office (FCO) travel advice on www.fco.gov.uk or call 0845 850 2829.

• Get travel insurance and check that the cover is appropriate and for your whole trip. Make sure it covers you for all activities, including hazardous sports. Take your policy number and the 24-hour emergency number with you.

• Check what vaccinations you need at least six weeks before you go. Check if your medication is legal in the country you are visiting and take a letter from your GP and your prescription.

• Check if you need to take extra health precautions, for example for malaria.

• Make sure your travel agent is an ABTA member and, if flying, that your holiday package is ATOL protected. If your trip involves flying on unfamiliar airlines, check their safety and reliability with a reputable travel agent.

• Get a good guidebook and get to know your destination. Find out about local laws and customs, especially relating to alcohol and drugs.

• Ensure you have a valid passport and necessary visas. Take another form of ID with you, preferably one with a photo.

• Make copies of your passport, insurance policy plus 24-hour emergency number, and ticket details – leave copies with family and friends.

• Take enough money for your trip and some back-up funds eg travellers cheques, sterling or US dollars.

• Leave a copy of your itinerary and a way of contacting you such as email, with family and friends.

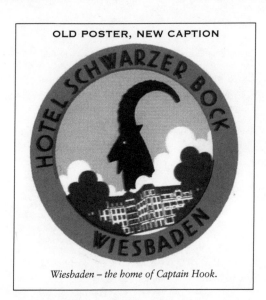

Wiesbaden – the home of Captain Hook.

DISTINCTIVE DWELLINGS

Train carriages, Tennessee, USA and York, England
All aboard for the land of Nod! The USA is king when it comes to wacky hotels, and the Chattanooga Choo-Choo is no exception. Stay in the opulent surroundings of a Victorian train and eat in the elegant dining car.

The Sidings Hotel in Yorkshire is a more intimate affair. Four carriages have been divided into two restaurants, a comfy lounge and eight bedrooms. You won't get very far, but your stay will certainly be more pleasant – and possibly cheaper – than the average train journey these days.

14 FEARS TO KEEP YOU AT HOME

Aerophobia	air, flying
Gephyrophobia	crossing a bridge
Dromophobia	crossing streets
Demophobia	crowds
Hypsophobia	high places
Acrophobia, altophobia	heights
Kinesophobia, kinetophobia	motion
Agoraphobia	open spaces
Topophobia	places
Xenophobia	strangers, foreigners
Hodophobia	travel
Siderodromophobia	travelling by train
Amaxophobia	vehicles
Basiphobia	walking

FANTASTIC FESTIVITIES

Wife Carrying Championships
Sonkajärvi, Finland, *July*

Contestants must carry a wife (not necessarily theirs)
round a 253.5m course of sand, grass, asphalt and water
obstacles: 15 points deducted for a dropped wife, the
wife's weight in beer for the winner.

International Regatta of Bathtubs
Dinant, Belgium, *August*

The fundamental rule of this (fundamental) nautical
festival is... yes, bathtubs. No motors are allowed, and
the influence of local businesses goes further than sponsoring the event – meat cleavers and other implements are
used to paddle the rafts. Contestants may douse each
other with buckets of water. However, rules forbid the
deliberate sinking of competitors.

CAN'T PULL, WON'T PAY

One Norwegian man's fruitless romantic pursuits during his holiday have inspired him to claim back its cost.

He has applied to his insurance company for compensation for the 'coldness of the pool', the £80 that was stolen from him and the general lack of sexual shenanigans. The very understanding Europeiske Reiseforsikring insurance company, used to bizarre demands, offered to help with the theft but declared: 'the ladies, he'll have to manage all by himself.'

ONE HUMP NOT TWO

Camel facts for the one humped dromedary

• Camels can travel for two weeks with no food or water.

• They can walk for 18 hours a day covering 20–25 miles.

• Pushed to their limits, they can travel over 100 miles a day.

• They have two toes which splay out to form a huge surface area to stop them sinking in the sand.

• Before setting out on a long journey camels are made to drink and store large quantities of water in their stomachs.

• After a long journey a camel can drink up to 30 gallons/136 litres/240 pints water at a single sitting.

• Fatty deposits in their humps are metabolised to provide nutrients and water during lean periods.

• They can lose a third of their body weight without harm.

• Although humans become ill if their body temperature rises more than 3.3°C (6°F), camels don't even sweat until their body temperature has risen 9°C (16°F) above normal.

• Dromedaries have been domesticated for 3,000 years – there are no truly feral camels now.

BATTLE OF THE BEACH

The culturally rich and interesting rivalry we have with our old friends the Germans is not something left behind when we head off on holiday, for it is precisely at these times that our paths seem to cross.

And let's face it, the tardy Brit who optimistically wonders down to the water expecting to find a really nice spot only to find rows of German holiday-makers laid out like cards in a game of pairs needs a little help. Now a holiday company has devised a towel territory rating table, covering all of Europe's top beaches, assessing each on its towel-to-person ratio. Measured by taking the size of a beach, dividing this by the size of the average towel, and then again by the average number of visitors, it's calculated that San Antonio on Ibiza is the Englishman's hardest target, with 1.1 towels per person. The Isla Canela, on the other hand, tucked away on the Costa de la Luz in southern Spain, has a whopping 14.5 towels per person, giving us a far higher chance of success.

However, choosing a beach and marking your territory is only half the battle. Suggested tactics thereafter include: making the children build sandcastles – apparently no one likes to trample such creations; putting up wind breaks and mini tents, however windy; erecting a large parasol; playing frisbee or bat and ball (don't hold back on the swing).

TRAVEL TEASERS

A train enters a tunnel at seven o'clock, another train enters the exact same tunnel, also at seven o'clock on the same day. The tunnel only has one track, and no other means for the trains to pass, around, over, or under. However, both trains made it to the other end of the tunnel untouched. How could this be?

Answer on page 144

SHARK ATTACK!

		Fatal Attacks	Total Attacks
1.	USA	69	855
2.	Australia	152	323
3.	South Africa	43	225
4.	Hawaii	19	99
5.	Brazil	20	78
6.	Papua New Guinea	31	65
7.	New Zealand	9	53
8.	The Bahamas	1	42
9.	Mexico	21	39
10.	Fiji Islands	10	25

A total of 2,000 attacks have been recorded since the 16th century by The International Shark Attack File. With 536 attacks, the 1990s saw the highest attack total, reflecting the rising popularity in aquatic activities.

COME SEE THE KHAMSEEN

Khamseen means 50; so called because this hot south-westerly Egyptian wind, coming from the Sahara, blows for about 50 days from April until June. The term was coined by the early Arabic speaking Christians to designate the period of days following Easter which lead to the feast of Pentecost, a Greek word meaning the 50th day. Khamseen is not originally the name of the storm but of the season during which these dusty winds are particularly abundant.

The same wind in the Sudan is known as Haboob. In Morocco it is called Chergui, Harmattan in Algeria, Chehili in Tunisia, Ghibli in Lybia – and for most westerners, it is simply the Sirocco.

LEFT OR RIGHT?

Curiously the Swedes, like all their neighbours, drove
on the right until 1736 when they decided to drive
on the left. In 1967, they decided to change back again,
so, in an ordered Scandinavian way, at 5am on Sunday
3 September they reverted back to the right-hand side of
the road. They stopped public transport for up to 24
hours so as not to confuse the issue. Soldiers were called
out to alter traffic lights and turn signs around. The
national speed limit was drastically reduced and raised in
small steps over the following months until it was back to
normal and everyone had got used to driving on the
right/wrong/right side of the road.

HOW GREEN IS MY VIKING?

After three years of exile spent exploring the coast of
Greenland, Erik the Red returned to Iceland in 986.
To entice Icelandic inhabitants to settle on the huge icy
island he had recently discovered, he somewhat distorted
the truth and named it Greenland! It worked.

According to the Sagas of Greenland, his son, Leif
Eriksson, a noble and sophisticated 'Golden' Viking, ven-
tured even further west and was the first European to try
to colonise the far North-east coast of the American continent. He landed on the shores of present day
Newfoundland, and called it Vinland, or Wine Land,
because of the red berries found there. However, the original colony of 35 did not remain there for long. By the end
of the 15th century, the settlements of the Norse peoples
in Greenland had withered away. Perhaps disease, the
local people or a mini ice age drove them away.

Great sea travellers, the Vikings ranged far across the
North Atlantic, keeping memories of their adventures
alive by their tradition of oral storytelling.

Fill your water bottle at night with hot tea. Put it in a sock. Put that down your sleeping bag and you have: a hot water bottle; warm, dry socks; and tea with which to brush your teeth in the morning.

Purified water's not that tasty: an effervescent vitamin tablet in your drinking water takes the bad taste away.

Large square handkerchiefs are multi-purpose: not only useful for blowing the lining of your nose into at high altitude, you can also protect the back of your neck from the sun, and wrap them round your face in dust storms.

If you wash your knickers and socks but don't have time to dry them, pin them on your daypack and they'll dry in the sun by lunch. Remember to pack lots of nappy pins, which not only make good roadside presents, but come in handy in many unexpected ways – for instance pinning drying laundry to your pack.

Energy tablets are very boring, repetitive, and so high in citric acid that in large doses they give you as bad an upset stomach as some trekking food. Pack tasty alternatives such as dried fruit or Biltong, strips of meat that are salted and dried in the sun.

Trekking food can be very plain: take with you things to spice up the offered fare – marmite and brown sauce (in unbreakable plastic containers) can make all the difference to a tasteless steamed vegetable dumpling.

TRAVEL TEASERS

A car's odometer shows 72,927 miles, a palindromic number. What are the minimum miles you would need to travel to form another?
Answer on page 144

OUTSTANDING AIRPORTS

King Khalid International Airport in Riyadh, Saudi Arabia is the largest airport in the world at 87 square miles. By comparison, London Heathrow is 4.7 square miles.

Atlanta's Hartsfield Jackson airport is the busiest in terms of passengers, handling close to 80 million passengers a year, but London Heathrow is the busiest in terms of international passengers (many US flights are domestic).

London is the busiest city in aviation terms – with Heathrow, Gatwick, Stansted, Luton and London City combined, it handles a total of almost 120 million passengers annually.

FOOD FJORDS

The Norwegians are a hospitable people. Along the ancient trails and trekking routes through their forests are many comfortably appointed huts in which the passing traveller is welcome to stay the night – on the understanding that they leave the hut tidy and as well equipped as it was when they arrived. So, for instance, if you arrive to find there's coffee, ham and cheese, you're welcome to these as long as you replace them before you leave.

TRAVEL TIPS

When presented with a landing card or visa application, think hard before you claim to practice an unusual profession. It's not always a good idea to say you're self-employed. Countries are nervous of people who might end up costing them money, so it can be worth calling yourself a secretary when you are in fact a journalist or a photographer.

Toad, from *The Wind in the Willows*, was just one of many for whom the advent of the motor car stimulated dreams of great travel...

By the early 20th century, there were over 8,000 motor vehicles in the US alone. In August 1907, Prince Borghese of Italy won the 8,000-mile Peking to Paris motor race in 62 days, overcoming problems from a bush fire to a Belgian policeman who booked him for speeding, in order to win his prize.

In 1908, the French paper *Le Matin* staged the first around the world car race. It was won by an American Thomas vehicle which took 170 days to cover the 13,500-mile course. The six car competition took place in an era when paved highways were almost unknown: there were no road maps, tires were fragile and cars frail. Six cars and a score of men took part. The only American car to compete was the winning Thomas Flyer.

Steep gradients were apparently no problem to the early motorist – in 1911, the first driver topped Ben Nevis, Britain's highest peak at 4,406ft.

Ian Fleming's fantasmagorical *Chitty Chitty Bang Bang* was inspired by a car built in 1920 by a certain Count Zborowski on his estate near Canterbury. His car's vast engine was encased in a grey steel body with a polished hood eight feet long. She weighed over five tonnes – in spite of which she managed to win the 1921 Brooklands 100mph short handicap at 101 miles per hour.

The Paris–Dakar Rally pits over 400 drivers against one another in a gruelling 17-day race over 6,500 miles. Competitors race all sorts of off road vehicles over the toughest terrain and conditions. The Paris–Dakar originated in 1978, a year after Thierry Sabine got lost in the desert and decided it might be a good place for a rally.

OLD POSTER, NEW CAPTION

As she felt its gentle twang for the 17th time, Carmen wondered what Carlos' over-familiar guitar would look like wrapped around his fat grinning face.

FANTASTIC FESTIVITIES

Tunarama, Port Lincoln, South Australia, *January*
This fish festival originated to celebrate the town's fish industry, which is centred on the tuna. The highlight of the annual January festival is the world championship tuna-tossing event where the city turns out to watch hearty men and women try and hurl the fish as far as possible.

CALM BEFORE THE STORM

The Pacific Ocean is known for some of the most powerful storms in the world, producing swells in excess of 100ft high. The first westerner to sail its treacherous waters in 1519, Ferdinand Magellan had the remarkable luck to cross it without encountering any storms at all! So he misnamed it Mar Pacifico (the calm sea). Magellan was killed fighting for a friendly native king in the Philippines in 1521 but one of his ships, under the captainship of a certain Juan Sebastian del Cano, made it back to Spain, so completing the first circumnavigation of the globe in 1522.

WELCOME ABOARD

The first ever air hostess was called Ellen Church and was employed by Boeing Air Transport. She was no trolley dolly though: she was hired for her nursing skills rather than her ability to serve customers. She applied to be a pilot, but the traffic manager of BAT was more keen on hiring her as a nurse to calm passengers as although air travel was becoming more common, most thought it too dangerous to even try.

Ellen became a stewardess on 15 May 1930 and worked the route between Oakland and Chicago. Stewardessing soon took off (pun intended) and many airlines boasted inflight service.

The requirements were very strict: a stewardess had to be a registered nurse; single; under 25; weigh less than 8 stone 2oz; and be less than 5ft 4in. This was largely motivated by the small size of early aircrafts which had narrow aisles, low ceilings and could not carry extra weight. The stewardesses were required to haul luggage, fuel planes and help pilots push planes into hangars as well as serve the passengers with sandwiches and coffee.

AIR WAYS

All airports are abbreviated to a three letter code:
just so you know where you are...

JFK	John F Kennedy – New York
JKT	Jakarta – Indonesia
LHR	London – Heathrow
LGW	London – Gatwick
LCY	London – City airport
LPL	John Lennon – Liverpool
BQH	Biggin Hill – UK
SFO	San Francisco – USA
MOW	Sheremetyevo 2 – Moscow
THR	Teheran
WOL	Wollogong – Australia
ZAG	Zagreb
LAX	Los Angeles

NO PLACE LIKE NOME?

The town of Nome in Alaska is so called because an
Alaskan-British map dated 1850 was misread – what the
map actually said was 'Name?' Nome had its heyday during the Gold Rush of 1898, which brought 20,000 people
to the area when it was found that even the sand on the
beach had gold scattered in it. A railway was built to
Nome in 1900 and the town is still there, in spite of a fire
in 1934 which destroyed most of the buildings from the
Gold Rush era. Now Nome's known as a start-out point
for visiting Alaska's glorious wilderness – on which the
miners' shovels and panning equipment can still be found.
Nome has also been commemorated in a Pixar animation
short film entitled *Knick Knack* (1989) which stars a
snowman in a snowglobe labelled Nome, Alaska. The film
appears on the DVD of *Finding Nemo* (2003), a film about
a little fish whose name, oddly, is an anagram of Nome.

What is it about Cuba that draws so many...?

Ernest Hemingway's *The Old Man and the Sea* opens in Havana.

In 1946, mobster Lucky Luciano called a summit in Havana. The meeting was held at the Hotel Nacional, the hotel famously built with Mafia money. The meeting was attended by a who's who of mobsters – Meyer Lansky, Frank Costello, Tommy Lucchese, Vito Genovese, Joe Bonanno, Santo Trafficante Jr and Moe Dalitz. Among the topics for discussion was the assassination of gangster Bugsy Siegel.

In 1946, Frank Sinatra made his singing debut in Havana.

On 10 December 1959, the Hotel Riviera opened in Havana. It cost US$14 million to build and most of the money was supplied by the Cuban government (the old Batista regime – Castro hadn't quite seized power yet) to the owner Meyer Lansky. The floor-show in the Copa Room was headlined that night by Ginger Rogers. Lansky wasn't impressed: he was heard to say that Rogers 'can wiggle her ass, but she can't sing a goddamn note.'

Guantanamo Bay was originally a holiday resort, and was leased to the US Navy in 1898. The terms of the lease require Washington to pay rent which was set a century ago at 2,000 gold coins a year, rent which is now worth a very good US$4,000. The lease can only be voided by mutual agreement or abandonment of the land by the US.

The Buena Vista Social Club, that lovely lazy sounding salsa band, comes from Santiago in Cuba, a place where music surrounds you all day. Even the lift attendant in the Ambos Mundos hotel (where Hemingway used to stay) in Havana will dance with you if there's a gap in the need for the lift.

TRAVEL TIPS

Make sure you take a large bottle of water with you when flying since air travel is one of the most dehydrating activities known to man. You should drink approximately 120 millilitres every hour and avoid alcohol, as it will only dehydrate you further. Applying moisturiser can also help prevent dry skin.

MIRACULOUS SURVIVOR

On 8 October 1568, Job Horton was set on land somewhere in the Bay of Mexico where he was taken prisoner by the Spanish. He recorded the next 23 years of his life as follows:

I suffered imprisonment in Mexico, two years.
In the Contractation House in Seville, one year.
In the Inquisition House in Triana, one year.
I was in the galleys, twelve years.
In the everlasting prison remediless, with the coat with St Andrew's cross on my back, four years.
And at liberty I served as a drudge Hernando de Soria three years, which is the full complement of 23 years.
Since my departure from England until this time of my return I was five times in great danger of death, besides the many perils I was in in the galleys.

First, in the port of St John de Ulua, where being on shore with many other of our company, which were all slain saving I and two other that by swimming got aboard the Jesus of Lubeck.
Secondly, when we were robbed by the wild Indians.
Thirdly after we came to Mexico, the Viceroy would have hanged us.
Fourthly, because he could not have his mind to hang us he would have burnt us.
Fifthly, the General that brought us into Spain would have hanged us at sea.
Thus, having truly set down unto you my travails, misery and dangers, endured the space of 23 years, I end.

SOME TRAVELLERS FROM YESTERYEAR

1. Marco Polo
(1254–1324) A Venetian merchant and adventurer, Marco Polo spent more than 20 years journeying from Europe to China, and his accounts have become classic travel literature.

2. Christopher Columbus
(1451–1506) Of Genoese origin, it was under the King and Queen of Spain's patronage that he arrived in the Caribbean instead of India, being one of the first Europeans to 'discover' the Americas.

3. Vasco de Gama
(1460–1524) A Portuguese navigator who opened up a new sea route from Europe to Asia via the Cape of Good Hope in Southern Africa, helping Portugal to become a world power.

3. Ferdinand Magellan
(1480–1521) Magellan, a Portuguese navigator and explorer, was the first to circumnavigate the globe. Starting from Spain, he reached South America, and crossed the Pacific via the Magellan Strait, as it's now known, to the Philippines.

5. Sir Francis Drake
(1540-1596) It took Drake, an English navigator, three years to successfully complete Magellan's voyage, arriving home in a ship brimming with exotic spices and treasures.

ALL CHANGE!

Borders where you have to pull over and drive
on the opposite side of the road:
The bridge over the Mekong: You drive on the left in
Thailand; the right in Laos.
The right in China; at the border with Pakistan, there's a
sign saying: 'Entering Pakistan. Drive on left'.
The left in Hong Kong; the right in China
The left in Namibia; the right in Angola
The right in Zaire; the left in Uganda

TRAVELLING WITH A CONSCIENCE

• Travelling is part of modern life but the consequences on the environment can be huge. Here are some of the negative effects of travelling, and what you can do to reverse the trend:

• 42% of a hotel's energy use is used on heating water, yet the majority of guests are willing to use their sheets and towels for more than one day. Use hotels that use a 'no change' policy or write your own note to the chambermaid.

• When on holiday, much of the money tourists spend does not go to the local people but to large tour operators, hotels and on imported food and drink. For every £100 spent on a holiday in a developing country, only around £5 actually stays in the country's economy. With so many developing countries relying on tourism for income, try and spend locally on hotels, goods and food.

• Water is a big issue in travelling. When abroad, the average tourist can use over 800 litres of water in 24 hours. Try and conserve water while you are travelling and encourage your hotel to introduce water saving techniques.

• Aviation produces more carbon dioxide than all human activity in Africa. And one long-haul return flight can produce more CO_2 per passenger than the average motorist produces in a year. One way to offset this trend is to pay voluntary tax at airports, for example at Luton where the money goes towards planting trees around the town to help soak up the carbon emissions from the planes.

TRAVEL TEASERS

What travels round the world but always remains in a corner?
Answer on page 144

KNOT MANY PEOPLE KNOW THIS

In times gone by, a captain would calculate his ship's speed by throwing a wooden log into the water and observing how fast it moved away from the ship. This approximate method of ship speed measurement was called 'Heaving the Log' and was used until the mid-1600s when the 'Chip Log' method was invented, probably by Dutch sailors.

The 'Chip Log' apparatus consisted of a small, weighted wood panel that was attached to a reel of rope and a half-minute sand glass. The rope had knots tied at equal distances along its length. Sailors would throw the wood panel into the sea and the rope would start unwinding from the reel. The faster the ship was moving the faster the rope would unwind. By counting the number of knots that went overboard in a given time, they could calculate the ship's speed. And that is the origin of the nautical speed unit: the knot.

So, how fast is a knot? It is equivalent to the nautical mile, which is 1.15 miles/hr or 1.85km/hr.

FANTASTIC FESTIVITIES

Reveillon, Rio de Janeiro, Brazil, *December*
Every December the people of Rio pay tribute to the goddess of the sea, Yemanja. General festivities of dancing and chanting lead up to the launching of tiny boats and baskets with offerings aboard. Popular gifts for the sea goddess include perfume, combs, mirrors, fried fish and watermelon.

If the gifts are carried out to sea, the boat owner will see good luck, but if the waves wash the offerings back ashore, the worshippers' prayers will be ignored.

NATURAL REMEDIES

The world over western medicine is being given new ideas by the traditional medicines used by indigenous peoples:

- Pineapples, used for medicinal purposes by the Guarani Indians of Brazil and Paraguay, contain an enzyme which could prevent thrombosis.
- The cancer-curing potential of the rosy periwinkle was brought to the attention of western scientists by the traditional healers of Jamaica and Madagascar.
- In Sarawak, Borneo, people use the 'tuba akar' plant to cure fever. The plant is also a useful fish poison.
- *Chinchona officinalis*, first used by South American Indians to cure fevers is now a source of quinine for the treatment of malaria.
- Australian Aborigines use the sap, leaves and bark of gum trees to control bleeding and to treat burns, wounds, cuts and bites.
- The dragon tree of the Canary Islands can grow to great heights and live for thousands of years.

It secretes a sap called dragon's blood which the locals, a people called the Guanches, used to staunch the flow of blood. You can still see dragon trees: near Icod, a village on Tenerife, stands an immense example, probably the oldest in the Canaries. It's less easy to find Guanches – as a people they were discovered when the Spanish first arrived on the Canary Islands. They lived a stone-age existence, sheltering in caves, dressing in goat skins and eating cheese and a kind of flour. They didn't know about metal but still managed to fight off the marauding Spaniards for nearly a century before, decimated by their enemies, plague and famine they died out.

- Closer to home, willow bark is an ancient European remedy, the properties of which are the basis of Aspirin, one of the world's oldest recognised analgesics.

GUIDE TO APPROPRIATE CLOTHING

1. DESERT
Where: Africa: Sahara, Kalahari; Australia: Simpson; Oman: Empty Quarter
Protection from the sun

What
• Long-sleeved cotton shirts and trousers, some of which now have sun protection factors.
• Sunscreens, neckerchiefs, wide-brimmed hats, sunglasses, sometimes even goggles, suede or fabric 'desert shoes', with thick soles and breathability, fibre-pile jacket, warm hat for cold nights.

2. TROPICAL
Where: Malaysia, Amazonia, Indonesia, Congo, Madagascar
Protection from leeches and rain

What
• Jungle boots or canvas baseball boots, with leech-proof vents where water can drain; spare pair will be needed if journey is likely to last more than a few months.

• Loose, light cotton clothing, not military patterned!, poncho, soft hat and bandana to keep sweat and leeches off your face; keep spare dry set in sealed waterproof bag.
• Knee-length socks, tightly woven and strong seams to prevent leeches from coming in, insect repellent and a leech-stick (a piece of wood with salt), some clothing is already impregnated with it.

3. MOUNTAIN
Where: Himalayas, Alps, Andes, Alaska, New Zealand, Pamirs (Tajikistan), Karakoram (Pakistani Himalayas)
Protection from the cold

What
• Flexible layering system: fast-dry synthetic base, fleece mid-layer, waterproof and breathable shell.
• No cotton, wide-hat, sunglasses, umbrella, fleece hat and gloves.
• Boots, either leather or fabric, with ankle protection, thick tread and midsole.

4. SOUTH POLE

Protection from freezing cold, your own sweat

What

• Synthetic long-johns, long-sleeved top, wind-proof fleece jacket, ventile sledging jacket (the first weatherproof/breathable jacket), fibre-pile salopettes (breathable material), waterproof/breathable nylon overtrousers.

• Inner gloves, waterproof, breathable outer mitts, thermal lightweight fleece mask, windproof head-band, inner and outer socks, plastic double boots, overgaiters to keep snow from entering tops of boots.

JOURNEY'S END

John Keats

John Keats died in Rome, of tuberculosis, in February 1821 aged 25. For the last few months of his life Keats lived in a room, the ceiling of which was painted with big white daisies on a blue background, in a dusty pink house, the Casina Rossa, at the foot of the Spanish Steps. His friend, the painter Joseph Severn, used to nip across the road to the Café Greco (still there) for 19th-century style takeaways, which he'd heat up on the fire in Keats's room.

Keats is buried in Rome's Protestant Cemetery. You can visit the room where he died, though all the original furniture in it was burned after his death on Papal orders.

DOCTOR WHO

The recommended traveller's first-aid box, according to the World Health Organisation, should include:

Adhesive tape • Antiseptic wound cleaner • Bandages • Emollient eye drops • Insect repellent • Insect bite treatment • Nasal decongestant • Oral re-hydration salts • Scissors and safety pins • Simple analgesic (such as para-cetamol) • Sterile dressing • Clinical thermometer

THE 10 MOST USEFUL LANGUAGES

Mandarin – 1,075 million speakers
English – 514 million speakers
Hindustani – 496 million speakers
Spanish – 425 million speakers
Russian – 275 million speakers
Arabic – 256 million speakers
Bengali – 215 million speakers
Portuguese – 194 million speakers
Malay/Indonesian – 176 million speakers
French – 129 million speakers

DISTINCTIVE DWELLINGS

Love Hotels, Japan

Many trips to Japan will result in accommodation with a difference. Visitors can stay in a traditional ryokan, or inn, where rooms are separated by sliding screen doors, tatami mats adorn the floors and guests sleep Japanese-style, on futons.

If claustrophobia isn't a problem for you, try a capsule hotel. Home of the travelling businessman on a budget, guests climb up into their own tubes, with barely enough room to sit up in bed.

For something really different try a Love Hotel. Love hotels offer privacy for couples usually forced to live in close proximity to the rest of their families, as well as for those looking for extra-marital antics. Rooms are available by the night or hour and check-in procedures are carried out via a computer in the lobby. There is enough entertainment in the rooms to keep you amused if you don't just have love on the mind: rooms come with karaoke, remote-control audio-visual systems and, an adventure in themselves, electronic toilets. You can find Love Hotels in every town, usually on the outskirts.

Cadillac Graveyard

In Bushland, Texas there are several Cadillacs sticking up out of the ground. The story behind this strange sight is that a rich oil tycoon once bought a brand new Cadillac which went to Cadillac heaven a bit sooner than he'd hoped. Said tycoon tried to get his money back but was refused. Such was his disgust that he decided to buy a brand new Cadillac every year and bury it in the ground on his vast property. As you do.

The Paper House

Rockport in Massachusetts can boast a rolled newspaper house. Well done them. Elis Stenman took newspapers and rolled them. And then he used them to design the interior walls of his house and build furniture. Over 20 years he stained and hardened huge amounts of newspaper to allow it to be used as furniture. From lamps, tables and chairs, Stenman even has a piano of paper.

Corn Palace

When your state boasts the impressive and much visited Mount Rushmore, how do you compete? Well the people of Mitchell, South Dakota are having a good go. They have taken the rather obvious choice of constructing a Corn Palace, a building structured like a castle, and every year since 1892 they staple different colours of corn cobs onto the building, creating pictures like Indians around a fire, or a horse and carriage. Ah, that old chestnut.

The tallest thermometer in the world

Ever had trouble reading the tiny scale on a regular sized thermometer and wondered if they could make it just a little bit bigger? Well they have – and not just a bit bigger. The world's tallest thermometer is based in Baker, California and stands at 134ft high, a reminder of the highest temperature ever recorded in the US at nearby Death Valley in 1934.

'One small step for a man,' uttered William H Braindead
on his maiden voyage, 'one giant leap for
maaaaaaaaaaaaaaah…'

LEFT OR RIGHT?

Exceptions to the rules

The Parnell Bridge in Cork, Ireland: you drive over on the right.

The Ponte Palatino and the Ponte Pietro Nenni in Rome, Italy: you drive over on the wrong side.

The Parc des les Cascades in Barcelona, Spain: you drive around on the left.

Savoy court, off the Strand, London, UK: you drive on the right. This is not only the main entrance to the hotel, but also to the theatre. The rule was instituted in 1929 so that cars queue-ing to drop people at the theatre wouldn't block access to the hotel.

In Canada, on Route 20, the Lachine rapids near Montreal: crossing bridges allow you to change back into the natural right-hand flow at each end.

Interstate 5 into LA from the north: you drive on the left.

When Argentina invaded the Falkland Islands the islanders were forced to drive on the right. However, this situation was soon reversed.

CHANGING WITH THE TIMES

In 1895 the *Times of London* produced a new atlas for Great Britain. Regarded as the best in the world at the time, German cartographers drew up the 118 maps. The atlas included a map of the solar system and the move-ments of planets and moons. Half the plates in this first edition concentrated on Europe. A second edition was needed to show the political changes after World War I. In this edition Europe only took up a third of the plates. In the atlas printed in 1955–1959, after World War II, Europe was given even less pages as European colonial power waned. *The Times Atlas* has been revised and updated and republished at regular intervals ever since.

TRAVEL TIPS

Money

In third world countries, it's often difficult to buy the currency before you get there. When you do, ask for lots of small denomination notes since outside large cities things will be very cheap and locals won't take kindly to being asked to change large notes.

Being armed with lots of small notes makes tipping easy too. American Dollars: a fistful of these will be welcomed in an emergency almost anywhere in the world.

Buy a cheap wallet and put some local coins in it and keep it in your pocket, for the pickpockets. You will then have protected your real money and the pickpocket will be none the wiser until it is too late. The cheap wallet will also give quick access to coins and small money you might need in a hurry without digging into your secret stash when in public.

SURVIVAL TIPS

Wreckage

If you've managed to escape an air accident, stay by the wreckage as this is where the rescuers will look first.

JUST AROUND THE CORNER

The 'four corners of the Earth' do not quite exist in a geographical reality. However, Cape Horn, at the tip of South America and Cape of Good Hope, at the tip of Africa, have been important navigational 'corners', helping European expansion and expeditions during the Age of Discovery. In religious terms, the 'corners' refer to the 'ends of the world', to which the disciples Paul and John travelled on their biblical missions.

WHEN IN ROME...

Some local taboos and laws it's worth brushing up on:

Turkmenistan: It is illegal to say anything bad about the Turkmen Dictator.

Korea: Triangles are considered a bad omen.

Chile: Avoid an open palm with separated fingers – it means 'stupid'.

China: Handkerchiefs are associated with weeping and funerals.

Japan: Nose blowing in public is not acceptable.

Saudi Arabia: Giving the thumbs up sign is considered very rude and offensive.

Greece, Turkey or Bulgaria: Nodding your head actually means no to some people.

Barbados: It's illegal for anyone, including children, to dress in camouflage clothing.

Fiji, and the Maldives: Topless bathing and nudity is forbidden.

Saudi Arabia: It is illegal for women to drive.

Thailand: You could serve 15 years in prison if you make critical or defamatory comments about the Royal family.

BRITISH CONSULATES CANNOT...

...get you out of prison

...give legal advice

...get you better treatment in hospital than the locals are given

...investigate a crime

...pay your hotel, legal, or other bills

...pay your travel costs except in exceptional circumstances

...do travel agent's, airline's, bank's or car hire company's jobs

...find you somewhere to live, a job or a work permit

TRAVEL TEASERS

Travelling to a city, you lose your way. You come to a
fork in the road and don't know which road to take.
Standing at the fork are two men. Next to the men is a
sign, which you may assume is correct, which states that
one of the two men always tells the truth and the other
always tells lies (but it is not known which is which).
  The sign goes on to say that travellers can only ask
one of the men one question. What question can you
pose that will give you the information you need to
choose the correct road?

Answer on page 144

JOURNEY'S END

Lady Jane Digby

Born in Dorset into the aristocratic Digby family in 1807,
the notorious and passionate beauty Lady Jane Digby
ended her days in Damascus in 1881 as the wife of a
Bedouin sheikh. She first married at 17 (the original Cad,
the politician Lord Ellenborough), escaped from him to
elope to Paris with an Austrian prince, then married a
German baron, and had affairs with, among others, the
King of Bavaria, a Corfiot count and an Albanian brigand
general. She finally found true love and happiness when
she married a Bedouin nobleman 20 years her junior. She
divided her time in Syria between the desert where her husband's tribe lived and Damascus where she had a beautiful
house in the garden of which she kept a menagerie of
exotic beasts. When in Damascus she used to spend some
evenings lounging on the roof of the explorer Richard and
Isobel Burton's house (he was the British consul in
Damascus at the time) smoking a narghile with them and
the famous Algerian rebel exile Abd el Kadir who also
lived there. She died at Damascus and is buried there.

Long periods of time spent sitting still in the cramped conditions of an airplane can cause deep vein thrombosis. To prevent this, invest in special support tights which are sold at airport shops, walk about as much as possible, and do the exercises recommended by airlines in their often highly entertaining videos shown around take off time. You could also take an aspirin before a long flight – aspirin thins the blood and so helps prevent clots.

Solar radiation increases dramatically between 30 and 50 thousand feet: so much so that during solar flare storms, airline pilots have been known to reduce their flight paths by 20,000ft to reduce their exposure to radiation. This annoys the airline companies as they're not able to use the jet stream and so save fuel.

Viruses love low humidity cabin air – which, as it is recycled, means one stands a good chance of picking up bugs. Should you wear a mask? There's no need to be too eccentric, but you might try drinking lots of water to prevent dehydration, keep off the booze and the coffee, eat all the fruit and fresh vegetables you can get hold of and you'll be in a better state to fight off infections floating about the cabin.

To fight air sickness, eat small regular meals, never have an empty stomach and you might invest in acupressure wristbands.

Ear problems in the air: never fly with a perforated ear drum. Ear ache when flying can be cured by swallowing. To induce swallowing in children, give them something to drink. To counteract ear popping, pinch nostrils and blow hard with mouth closed. Don't worry if you look silly: at least you'll take the minds of nervous flyers off their fears of take off and landing.

WHERE IS THE SAFEST PLACE
TO SIT ON AN AEROPLANE?

Some say the back is the safest, some say you should try and be far away from the engine. But the short answer is: there is no safest seat. Or at least not one that could be predicted before the accident. The place of impact can be the most important factor, but this is impossible to foresee. In some cases, for example in heavy smoke or fire, the ability to stay calm and remove yourself from the aircraft is much more important than where you are sitting.

GIVE THE WORLD A BREAK

Safaris and wildlife holidays
In the name of 'conservation', local people often find themselves cleared from their own land and wildlife relentlessly disturbed, so check the area for its sustainable tourism policies.

Sex tourism
Many children in South-east Asia are sexually exploited by tourists. There are now laws that prosecute offenders in the UK for crimes committed abroad, so report any unusual behaviour you have witnessed.

Off the beaten track?
Don't overly rely on your guidebook, you may end up in backpackers' paradise without having really visited the place. Instead, talk to the locals about their recommendations.

Sharing of cultures
Sharing photos and postcards from home is a good way of interacting with people abroad, exposing a bit of your culture in exchange.

Minimise using natural resources
Western travellers' habits are far more wasteful then local peoples and often have damaging effects on the environment, such as excessive water consumption and deforestation. So go easy on your hot showers and other standards.

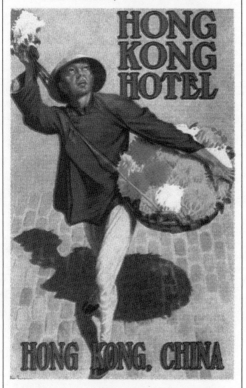

*Somebody had to get the tribbles off the Enterprise,
and Lt Sulu drew the short straw.*

SURVIVAL TIPS

Surviving in the desert

• Remember that it's possible to die of hypothermia during the night in even the hottest of deserts.

• Camel milk can be a powerful purgative.

• If you have water, ration it immediately you realise you're lost.

• Water holes are usually marked by large stones or brushwood but tend to be seasonal and are not always available.

• If you locate a dry stream bed, dig at the lowest point you can find on the outside bend and you might find water.

• Never dig during the heat of the day as you will sweat more liquid than you're likely to find and you might collapse with heat exhaustion.

• Because of the extremes of temperature in the desert, water condensation using polythene traps can be a good way of gathering water during the night.

• If you have to walk to safety only walk at night: during low night temperatures you can cover as much as 25 miles: if you walk during the day you're unlikely to get further than five miles before collapsing.

• In hot desert temperatures of 40–50°C you need eight pints of water per person per day for healthy kidney function.

• If waiting for rescue, wait in the best shade you can find: under a ground sheet or in the shade of a vehicle and avoid sitting on hot ground.

• To make fires, camel droppings make good fuel.

• Don't strip off your clothes: not only will you burn but you'll lose more water through perspiration than if you keep clothes on.

• In strong sun always keep your neck and head covered because the brain is very sensitive and cannot tolerate over-heating.

HIGH-DE-HIGH

The first stories of altitude sickness came from a party
led by Diego de Ordas, a conquistador, who climbed the
volcano Popocatépetl, 60 miles from modern Mexico city,
in 1520. At 5,452m, it was the highest mountain climbed
to that date, and remained the highest climbed until the
conquests of the first Himalayas.

WORDS THAT TRAVELLED FAR

Turkey	kiosk
Greece	tonic
South Africa	trek
Greenland	anorak
India	mulligatawny
Canada	toboggan
Czech Republic	pistol
Czech Republic	robot
Serbo Croatia	cravat
Ital	balcony
Italy	banana
Spain	cannibal
Holland	poppycock

TRAVEL TIPS

Sarongs and pashminas make useful travelling compan-
ions. Light, and folding up to practically nothing, they're
easy to carry at the bottom of a day-pack. Should you
find yourself in shorts longing to visit a temple where
habitual European hot weather semi-nakedness is frowned
upon, they make a good skirt. They are also handy as protection from the sun, as a light shawl, a blanket on aero-
planes, an extra pillow or as a bundle in which to tie up
loot you've spent the afternoon haggling over in a bazaar.

THE STREETS ARE PAVED WITH...
BASALT

The world's oldest paved road is reported to be in Egypt, 43 miles south-west of Cairo. The eight-mile stretch of basalt pavement was built sometime between 2625 and 2250 BC. The road was used to transport blocks of basalt from a quarry to a quay on the now evaporated Lake Moeris. The road was an average of only six feet across and each side of the road was paved with slabs of sandstone and limestone. The basalt was loaded onto barges and carried across the lake to where it joined the River Nile, a connection possible only during the river's annual summer flood. Basalt was an important road material at the time and was used in the construction of many roads. It symbolised the black, organic-rich soil of the Nile flood plain that made Egyptian civilisation possible.

OLD POSTER, NEW CAPTION

Tucson – birthplace of the old 'arrow-through-the-head' gag.

TRAVEL TEASERS

Rearrange the letters of an African country to make a South American capital.
Answer on page 144

MAP-MAKING MAGIC

According to Ptolemy, a Greek mathematician and geographer: maps are able to 'exhibit to human understanding... the earth through a portrait'. He drew up a map-makers manual on how to convert the three-dimensional surface of the globe into a two-dimensional map. It was handed down for 1,500 years among map-makers until the Renaissance where it was converted to print, spurring mass circulation.

Gerard Mercator, (1512–1594), an educated geographer living in Antwerp, then the centre of commerce, took this manual to heart and set out to become the 'Prince of modern geographers'. By 1541, he realised the world's largest printed globe, which won him the patronage of Emperor Charles V. Despite brutal incarceration by the Inquisition in 1543 triggering a decade of no production, he managed to produce up to 107 revolutionary maps by the end of his life. He pioneered the systematic use of mathematical grids of longitude and latitude, and the overlapping of adjacent cartographic regions, which seams the entire planet together on a map. He can also boast coining the term 'atlas' after his collection of maps, and pinpointing the magnetic pole.

DISTINCTIVE DWELLINGS

Treehouses, Hawaii

Want to hush-a-bye baby, on the tree-top? Then the tropical forests of Hawaii are the place to go. The Tree house of the August Moon, on Maui, perches 10ft above the ground in African tulip trees. It has living and sleeping areas, a kitchen, and a balcony complete with hammocks.

There is a flush toilet and hot shower in a separate bamboo 'bathroom', but no electricity.

GIVE THE WORLD A BREAK

The sanctity of tribal communities

If determined to visit tribal communities, only do so in the presence of their own guides and do not encourage tourist resorts to exploit traditional rituals for entertainment sake.

Trekking and camping

Misuse of mountain paths, driving off-road, camping outside of sites, littering and building fires disturb both nature and wildlife, so be mindful when enjoying the beauties of nature.

Bargaining or haggling?

There is a fine line between bargaining and forcing a vendor to actually lose profit out of desperation, so be graceful and remember that your budget is still far greater than theirs.

Endangered species and souvenirs

While no one directly supports poaching, by buying illegal animal products made from the CITES list of endangered species, you are contributing to their disappearance.

Public displays of affection

Body language is interpreted in as many different ways as there are countries, so refrain yourself from being overtly affectionate with your partner, friends and locals alike.

DO'S AND DON'TS WHEN TRAVELLING ABROAD

Do take your shoes off before entering a house in Japan
Don't show the soles of your feet in Nepal
Don't accept the third cup of coffee from a Bedouin
Do shake hands with a Frenchman
Don't stand too close to an Englishman in a queue
Don't come to the point too quickly in Saudi Arabia
Do belch after a good meal in Belgium
Don't eat with your left hand in any country where
you eat from a central dish

JOURNEY'S END

Percy Bysshe Shelley

Drowned in July 1822, in a boating accident in the Gulf of La Spezia off the coast of Liguria. In the Keats-Shelley house in Rome there's a watercolour of his body being cremated there. His ashes are buried in the Protestant Cemetery in Rome along with his friends Keats and Severn.

MALARIA – NOT SO TRIVIAL TRIVIA

- Present in 100 countries

- Over 10,000 travellers a year fall ill after their return home from a malarial destination.

- Symptoms can take up to three months to appear.

- Malaria is caused by a Protozoan parasite called *Plasmodium* of which there are four malaria species: *P. vivax, P. falciparum, P. ovale, P. malariae* – all these are carried by the anopheles mosquito which bites mainly at dusk and night time.

- Malaria always takes at least seven days to incubate.

- The most severe Malaria is the one caused by *P. falciparum*. Its symptoms include: fever, headache, chills, muscle weakness, aching, vomiting, cough and diarrhoea and it can well be fatal if not treated within 24 hours of symptoms commencing.

Z IS FOR...

Zanzibar, Tanzania
Zion National Park, Utah, US
Zambia
Zürs, Austria
Zakynthos, Greece

Zhejiang, China
Zermatt, Switzerland
Zagora, Morocco
Zamora, Peru
Zennor, Cornwall, England

Henry leant forward for just a second, but it was all it needed to ruin yet another painting.

TRAVEL TEASERS

A man goes for a walk. He walks south one mile, east one mile, and north one mile, and ends up in the same place he started. But the place is not the north pole. Where is it?

Answer on page 144

Flying can be a bit of an expense for the enthusiastic traveller who wants to jet around the world. If only flying was free... One man realised this dream: David Phillips from California managed to accumulate enough air miles to never have to buy a flight again. But he didn't get them in a conventional way.

David noticed a promotion on Healthy Choice frozen meals that meant you could claim 500 air miles for every 10 Universal Products bar codes you collected. This got David thinking. He scoured the supermarket and hit gold when he found individual servings of pudding for just 25 cents, each with their own barcode. He cleaned out the supermarket of pudding. And the warehouse. And then he phoned the distributors and located every shop that was in his area. David visited 10 stores and cleaned them all out of pudding. When he finished he had 12,150 servings of pudding but soon realised he had only a little time left before the offer ran out and no way of tearing off all the barcodes in time. Not one to give up on an idea, David hit upon the idea of donating all the pudding to a local food bank for the Salvation Army who agreed to tear off all the labels in return for the donation. And so he had his barcodes.

David sent them off, hoping that he would not be disqualified on a technicality, and soon the air mile certificates started to pour in – 1,253,000 miles in all. And because he had passed the million mile mark he was also upgraded to Gold Status, meaning he had a special reservations number, priority booking, upgrades and bonus miles.

David has become a cult hero – the man who made good, who saw a loophole and beat the big guys without breaking the rules.

The story was the inspiration behind the 2003 film *Punch Drunk Love* starring Adam Sandler and Emily Watson.

World's largest peanut

This nutty monolith is a whopping 10ft long and stands atop a 15ft pillar in Ashburn, Georgia. It was erected in 1975 as a memorial to Nora Lawrence Smith, member of the Georgia Journalism Hall of Fame and co-publisher of the *Wiregrass Farmer*. Perhaps she loved peanuts. Or perhaps she just has some very odd relatives.

Spam Museum

Ah spam, that centrepiece of haute cuisine and every child's fantasy food. Previously overlooked, it is now celebrated in Austin, Minnesota at the Spam Museum. Thank the lord. It is a remarkable 16,500 sq ft and promises to introduce you to the world of spam through videos, fun exhibits and educational games.

Cranberry World

The cranberry is well ingrained in American culture, being the traditional accompaniment to Thanksgiving turkey. And so, to celebrate the berry, what better way than to build a museum? Plymouth in Massachusetts obviously had the same thought and so Cranberry World was born. You can learn all about the cranberry and ruminate on such facts as: 20% of all cranberries in the US are consumed in the fourth week of November.

Albino Squirrels

Pretty rare, albino squirrels. And even rarer, a town claiming to be the sole habitat of such pasty pets. However, there's not one but five towns vying for the honour of being albino squirrel capital of the world. Olney, Illinois; Marionville, Missouri; Kenton, Tennessee; Brevard, North Carolina; and Exeter, Ontario – each claims to be the 'real' albino squirrel centre and each has its own strange way of celebrating their pale pets. Olney has a law giving squirrels the right of way on the street, and Marionville captures common grey squirrels and throws them out of town.

NOT SO TALL AFTER ALL

Why Everest isn't actually the highest mountain in the world

Many of the thousands of islands in the Pacific Ocean, making up Micronesia and Polynesia, are formed by hot mantle plumes pushing up to the surface from deep in the earth's interior. When they reach the surface they form volcanoes. If these volcanoes are tall enough they stick out above the sea surface to form islands. The tallest of these is Mauna Kea in Hawaii at 4,205m above sea level. If this volcano were measured from its submarine base to its peak, it would be 10,203 m. This is taller than Everest which is only 8,846m!

HOTEL ALL THE WAY

'Born in a hotel room – and god damn it – died in a hotel room.' Eugene O'Neill, (1888–1953) US dramatist. He was born in a New York City Broadway hotel room. For much of his life he suffered from a debilitating Parkinson's-like disease. When he died in 1953, it was – much to his chagrin – also in a hotel room.

DISTINCTIVE DWELLINGS

Island Palace, Rajasthan, India

With the decline of the old ruling classes, many former palaces and castles have been converted into luxurious hotels. This ornate wonder was built in the 17th century as the summer resort of rulers of the Raj.

It's now a five-star hotel and guests can while away the hours by pools and fountains in cool courtyards, or dine under elegantly-carved white marble arches as the sun sets over the lake.

The answers. As if you needed them.

P7. India

P26. Montana

P32. Marco Polo and Mungo Park

P34. The boy, the older twin, was born on March 1. Then the boat crossed the International Date Line, and the girl was born on February 28. In a leap year, the younger twin celebrates her birthday two days before her older brother.

P48. Finland

P57. They were married, whereas everyone else was single.

P60. Congo

P68. The Tropic of Capricorn

P79. Nowhere, you don't bury survivors.

P82. Minnesota

P101. As they pass each other, they're both the same distance from New York City, no matter how far each has travelled.

P107. One entered at 7am, the other at 7pm

P110. 110 miles (73,037 miles)

P119. A stamp

P130. Ask one of the men what the other man would answer to the question: 'Is the left road the correct road?' Then assume the answer is false. If the man you ask is the liar, he'll incorrectly give you the truthful man's answer. If the man you ask is the truthful man, he'll correctly give you the liar's wrong answer.

P136. MALI – LIMA

P140. He started one mile north of the latitude in the southern hemisphere that is precisely one mile in circumference. Thus, when he walked the mile east, he went round a complete circle.

DURING THE COMPILATION OF THIS
BOOK, THE COMPANION TEAM...

Spent 327.6 hours daydreaming about exotic locations

Fell asleep on the train home six times and so travelled
a little further than intended

Visited seven different countries, and got drunk in six
of them

Received 12 postcards from friends and family
who were travelling

Stole four towels, and countless bottles of shampoo
from hotels

Set off the metal detector at the airport 14 times,
12 times because they forget to take their keys out of
their pocket

Purchased 17 useless souvenirs for relatives, eight of them
unidentifiable carvings

Worked out they had travelled to an average of
17 countries each and spoke seven languages between
them

Spent three hours arguing over who had had the worst
ever journey

Lost their passports six times

Found £62.37 of foreign currency lying around the house
(£26.88 of which is now obsolete)

Felt guilty about the towels, and posted two
of them back

*Please note that although every effort has been made to
ensure accuracy in this book, the above statistics may be
the result of wandering minds.*

TRAVEL NOTES, JOTTINGS,
IDEAS AND DOODLES

TRAVEL NOTES, JOTTINGS,
IDEAS AND DOODLES

TRAVEL NOTES, JOTTINGS,
IDEAS AND DOODLES

TRAVEL NOTES, JOTTINGS,
IDEAS AND DOODLES

TRAVEL NOTES, JOTTINGS,
IDEAS AND DOODLES

TRAVEL NOTES, JOTTINGS,
IDEAS AND DOODLES

TRAVEL NOTES, JOTTINGS, IDEAS AND DOODLES

TRAVEL NOTES, JOTTINGS,
IDEAS AND DOODLES

TRAVEL NOTES, JOTTINGS,
IDEAS AND DOODLES

TRAVEL NOTES, JOTTINGS,
IDEAS AND DOODLES

TRAVEL NOTES, JOTTINGS, IDEAS AND DOODLES

TRAVEL NOTES, JOTTINGS, IDEAS AND DOODLES

TRAVEL NOTES, JOTTINGS, IDEAS AND DOODLES

TRAVEL NOTES, JOTTINGS,
IDEAS AND DOODLES

THIS BOOK WOULD NOT HAVE BEEN POSSIBLE WITHOUT THE RESEARCH, IDEAS, AND DOGGED SUPPORT OF:

Sam Green-Armytage, Gemma Barnett,
Katie Braun, Ollie and Jules Campbell, Jessica Cardenas,
Gemma Clunie, Ed Dowding, Katherine Lawrey,
Naomi Pollard, Nick Smith,
Angharad, Douglas and Kay Guy,
Toby Wagstaff and Mike Woods.